Selected Quotes from

HUMAN TRAFFICKING:
From 5000 BC to the 21st Century

"The crime of human trafficking steals many years from a victim's life while subjecting sex slaves to unimaginable abuse and daily rape."

"Human trafficking is the third largest criminal activity in the world after illegal drugs and illegal weapons."

"Pimps, assuming they won't be caught, enslave children, women, and men."

"A Utah state lawmaker seeks a permanent penalty—death—for pimps and sex traffickers of children."

"As human trafficking increases we must turn our legal system on its head…instead of presuming innocence, let's presume guilt."

"Sadly, men of all ages, all colors, all walks of life, single and married, are buying and renting bodies of children and women for coerced sex (rape) and forced labor."

"From time immemorial, men have raped to subjugate and ejaculate, to sate their id and negate their superego—the conscience of the self."

"According to US Department of Justice in 2014, there were 400,000 untested rape kits gathering dust for years in police department storage facilities across America."

"Don't mess with Texas; you're lucky if you *only* do time."

Human Trafficking: from 5000 BC to the 21st Century

Human Trafficking: from 5000 BC to the 21st Century

7,000 YEARS OF SLAVERY, RAPE, GREED

K. G. Richardson
A Create/Space Book

© 2015 K. G. Richardson
All rights reserved.

ISBN: 1522978372
ISBN 13: 9781522978374
Library of Congress Control Number: 2016900031
CreateSpace Independent Publishing Platform
North Charleston, South Carolina

Because of the dynamic nature of the Internet, any web addresses or links contained in this book may have changed since publication and may no longer be valid. The views expressed in this work are solely those of the author and do not necessarily reflect the views of the publisher, and the publisher hereby disclaims any responsibility for them.

*For
the millions of
children, women, and men
who suffered and are still suffering
the loss of a life stolen from them*

Contents

Foreword	What Does Your DNA Reveal?	xi
Prologue	What Do You Know about Slavery?	xiii
Introduction	The Origins of Slavery and Human Trafficking	xv

Part One — White Slaves of the Ancient World 1

Preface	Early Slave Societies	3
Chapter 1	Democratic Athens? Centuries of Slavery; Decades of Democracy	5
Chapter 2	Imperial Rome: The Most Brutal Slave Society of Its Time	13
Conclusion	Times Change; Slavery Doesn't	25

Part Two — Black Slaves of the New World 27

Preface	Random Hazards of History	29
Chapter 3	The Enslavers: Africans, Arabs, Europeans, and Americans	31
Conclusion	Power Corrupts	63

Part Three	**Sex Slaves of Today's World**	·····65
Preface	Is She Your Missing Daughter?	·····67
Chapter 4	International Sex Trade	·····69
Chapter 5	International Rape Culture	·····83
Conclusion	Right Makes Might	·····95
Epilogue	Human Trafficking aka Slavery, Rape, Greed	·····97

Selected Bibliography ·····99
Acknowledgements ·····103
About the Author ·····105

FOREWORD
What Does Your DNA Reveal?

---

*White, black, brown, yellow, red—
no matter what your color, it's likely
that someone in your family, way back,
was once a slave.
For every corner of the earth has
known slavery. And every people on the
earth has been its victim.*

MILTON MELTZER
ALL TIMES, ALL PEOPLES

PROLOGUE

What Do You Know about Slavery?

I AM AN AMERICAN WHO read about slavery in high school in the early 1950s. But I paid little attention to this subject. After all, slavery in the United States had ended many decades earlier, when the Civil War was over in 1865. It is now 150 years since that war, and what do you know about slavery? Can you define *slave* in twenty words or less? Think about it. Write your definition down. Don't peek. Compare it with this one from *Webster's New World Dictionary*, Second College Edition (1972):

"A human being who is owned as property by another and is absolutely subject to his will."

Please remember this definition as you read this book.

As I got older, it bothered me that I knew so little about this dreadful part of our history. So I decided to learn more about slavery, not only in America but also in other parts of the world. What was slavery like thousands of years ago, and where does it exist today? Here's what I found:

White Slaves. Nearly *100 percent* of the slaves in the ancient world of Athens and Rome were white. Their unpaid labor created greater profits for their owners and built many public buildings for the government. Rape by slave owners was common.

Black Slaves. African kings, tribes, and nations enslaved each other for centuries, also for unpaid labor and coerced sex (rape). Then Arabs, Europeans, and Americans arrived and turned slavery and rape into a *profitable business around the world.*

Sex Slaves. Forced labor, including sexual slavery, in today's private economy generates *$150 billion in illegal profits* (US dollars) annually worldwide. The International Labour Organization (ILO) of the United Nations released this information on May 20, 2014. The ILO report said two-thirds, or $99 billion, came from commercial sexual exploitation.

Are you ready to go on a 7,000-year journey of discovery that reveals slavery, rape, and greed as accomplices in spawning modern slavery, known today as *human trafficking?* Human trafficking (HT) affects more than 140 countries, including America. You can help create a better tomorrow by understanding HT today…starting now.

INTRODUCTION

The Origins of Slavery and Human Trafficking

MANY HISTORIANS BELIEVE THAT SLAVERY began about 7,000 years ago in Mesopotamia, an area between the Tigris and Euphrates Rivers in modern-day Iraq. Whenever wars occurred, the winning tribe usually killed the losing men and enslaved their women, not only for work but also for coerced sex (rape). Surviving children were raised as slaves. As food became more plentiful, victors decided that enslaving, feeding, and putting defeated opponents to work was more useful than killing them. As long as they could control them, why not enslave them all and sell or trade some of them to other tribes for goods and money?

Slavery became a lucrative business of traders, sellers, buyers, and owners—yelling, pushing, shoving, and craning their necks—eager to see naked women, children, and men on the auction block ready for sale. Buyers forced open mouths of slaves to check their teeth, examined their ears, and fondled female breasts. They squeezed arm and leg muscles to feel how firm they were and ordered slaves to hop around, sometimes with feet fettered, to determine their stamina.

Some slave traders specialized in exhibiting young, nubile, attractive women in private to whomever could afford them and for whatever purpose they desired. These women fetched a high price and provided sellers with a sizable profit. Other traders offered young men with strong backs for work on farms—males who toiled from sunup to sundown and sometimes during the entire night, especially when the moon waxed full and flooded the fields with light. The profit on these slaves was also very good. Other traders sold older men of minimal strength and marginal endurance, who ended up working in mines and often died there. Although each older slave usually sold for a lower price and profit than a younger slave did, the traders still made a lot of money because older slaves were replaced more often.

Finally, there were the children. Some were born into slavery, raised in slavery, accustomed to slavery. Many were docile, malleable, easily controlled, and as easily trained as a dog or an ox. Every slave, young or old, had a use, and quite a few were worked hard until they wore out and died.

From Mesopotamia to Athens and then, much later, America, the business of slavery, rape, and greed has resulted in broken hopes, broken families, broken bones, and stolen lives. Very few people, other than slaves, cared about the well-being of a slave. Business was business to those in power; slaves were merely replaceable parts in an economic system that persists today as a profit-driven enterprise known as *human trafficking*, the world's third largest criminal activity after illegal drugs and weapons.

PART ONE

White Slaves of the Ancient World

PREFACE

Early Slave Societies

NEARLY ALL SOCIETIES IN THE history of the world owned slaves, which they acquired by either capturing or buying them. Does this mean they were slave societies? Not according to British historian Keith Hopkins, who stated the following in his book *Conquerors and Slaves*, published in 1978: "Only a handful of human societies can properly be called 'slave societies,' if by slave society we mean a society in which slaves play an important part in production and form a high proportion (say over 20%) of the population."

According to this definition, Athens and Rome can be considered slave societies, despite their well-chronicled achievements of being superior civilizations. Chapters 1 and 2 of this section look at the dark side of each society, revealing brutal practices that enslaved millions of people for thousands of years.

CHAPTER 1

Democratic Athens? Centuries of Slavery; Decades of Democracy

---

ANCIENT ATHENS WAS A SLAVE-OWNING society, ruled for more than three thousand years by kings, magistrates, and tyrants. During this long span, several elite citizens created a democracy that functioned intermittently from 508 to 322 BC. (This laudable attempt at democracy lasted only 186 years out of 3,000 years of early Greek history.) Wealthy landowners and the government owned the vast number of slaves before, during, and after this relatively short-lived democracy. Although the words *slave owning* and *democracy* seem to oppose each other, ancient Greeks did not view these terms as being contradictory.

The ancestors of today's Greeks settled the southeastern tip of the Balkans, a region serving as an ancient pathway and waterway between Europe and Asia. Native people grew up there, while others, perhaps seeking a new life, moved to the area from Western and Northern Europe and the Near East. Around 3000 BC, hunter-gatherers, probably from Asia Minor, came to this large, mountainous peninsula, washed by the Aegean and Ionian seas; these seas are part of the larger Mediterranean Sea.

The new residents arrived with sheep, goats, a variety of seeds to plant, and slaves. The newcomers mingled with the existing population to form farms and villages. Many roads connected these settlements with city-states on the mainland and on the islands around it; a few larger city-states included Sparta, Thebes, and Athens. During the next several hundred years, the Greeks expanded trade among the islands and with countries along the eastern Mediterranean, exchanging products for slaves.

Throughout history, people rose to positions of power due to birth, wealth, hard work, elective office, and violence. They assumed the role of aristocrats, otherwise known as the privileged class, the upper class, or the nobility. Members of these groups might also be referred to as *plutocrats*—wealthy people who worked together to influence and control the government, regardless of its structure.

Beginning in 1556 BC, seventeen kings, followed by numerous magistrates, ruled the city-state of Athens for more than one thousand years before it became a democracy in 508 BC. During these ten centuries, Athens grew stronger by merging with smaller settlements and conquering others. Throughout several wars, financial panics, and internal power struggles, one aspect of Athenian life remained the same: *the practice of slavery*. Rulers waged war to increase it. Plutocrats and businesses embraced it. Most inhabitants of Athens, even the slaves, seemed to accept it. Slavery was considered part of the human condition, whether Athens was a monarchy, a plutocracy, an aristocracy, or a very brief, sputtering democracy.

SOURCES OF SLAVES IN ANCIENT ATHENS

How did governments or businesses within various Greek city-states acquire slaves, these human tools of production? They relied on slave-trading merchants who bought captives from numerous slave-gathering people such as generals, admirals, and pirates. These slave-gatherers acquired their victims through various means, such as the following:

War. In the ancient world, more people became slaves after losing a war than any other way. When winners stopped killing defeated men on the battlefield, slave-trading merchants appeared at once to purchase captives. The merchants snapped them up at bargain prices because the victorious army, perhaps focusing on the next battle, did not want to be bothered with feeding or guarding its captives. The slaves sold later for much higher prices; in other words, the merchants bought low and sold high, maximizing their profits.

(Then, as now, markets are markets, whether in slaves or stocks. Investors or traders in securities or human bodies are eager to buy low and sell high. Today's human traffickers and pimps make use of these centuries-old business practices.)

Kidnapping and Piracy. Slave traders and kidnappers from around the Black Sea, Asia Minor, and the Grecian peninsula roamed the countryside looking for victims. Unfortunately, many captives were children, some sold by poor, desperate parents.

Piracy was a form of kidnapping on the high seas. Rowed by slaves and manned with warriors, pirate ships seized vessels, cargo, and people. They also raided coastal towns and cities. If some of the captives were wealthy, they demanded ransom. When the kidnappers did not get it, they sold these people and the rest of their victims into slavery.

In the ancient world, pirates took their prisoners to islands in the Aegean Sea, such as Delos, which had the capacity to detain and process ten thousand slaves at one time. Pirates would glide into port, unload their captives to eager buyers, collect their money, and leave quickly, presumably to seek more victims.

Birth. When a slave mother gave birth, the baby usually became a slave, regardless of whether the father was a free man or a slave. Many owners of large farms encouraged slaves to procreate, assuring a steady supply of new slaves while possibly increasing morale among male slaves. But some slave owners felt that slave breeding resulted in an economic disadvantage: mothers usually needed time off from work to ensure a safe delivery and care for the newborn baby. Other Athenian slave owners participated in slave breeding by raping the women.

Debt. In an agricultural society, such as ancient Athens, farmers lived at the mercy of nature and in fear of debt. If poor harvests resulted in little income, these farmers had to depend on neighbors, lenders, or the state. Dependence on moneylenders created debt slavery among farmers and others.

In 595 BC the people of Athens elected Solon as chief magistrate (archon). He cancelled debt slavery and became an instant champion of the masses, especially farmers. However, this act created a labor shortage. With fewer slaves, who would do the work? Athenian plutocrats had an answer: they imported more slaves from other countries.

Crime. In the ancient world, many societies, including Athens, enslaved criminals as punishment. Depending upon the severity of the crime, their sentence could be measured in decades or for life. Thieves often served their victims as slaves; sometimes the entire family of a convicted murderer could be enslaved to pay for the crime.

Slaves at Work in Ancient Athens

Slaves labored long hours without pay for private owners or the government in ancient Athens. Slaves worked as tools of production and distribution: slaves with hoes predated the plow; slaves with strong backs carried heavy loads long before the use of oxen or horses; slaves planted and picked crops for centuries before the development of mechanized farm equipment; slaves built public buildings, aqueducts, roads, weapons, and more for the state. Throughout Athenian history the unpaid labor of slaves contributed to increased private profits and large public projects.

Depending upon their education and skills, most slaves labored in one of five major work environments: mines, farms, households, workshops, or services. This latter category included various governmental services and departments. Private slave owners dominated the first four environments, while the state controlled the fifth. Large landowners hired overseers to supervise their slaves, permitting the owners to devote time and energy to recreation, the arts, and politics. Many of these aristocratic slave owners eagerly discussed ideas of democracy, liberty, and freedom among themselves, but it apparently never occurred to them that these concepts contradicted their continued practice of slavery. Slavery was the accepted norm; it had existed as part of Greek life for centuries. The plight of slaves mattered very little to owners.

Mines. Aristotle reportedly stated that a slave's life had three elements: work, punishment, and food. Hundreds were pushed to exhaustion, flogged, and ill fed as they labored in a silver mine twenty-five miles from Athens. Their ten-hour workday (that's about how long each slave's oil lamp lasted) began early in the morning with some bread that provided just enough energy to get them through the day. The slaves washed down the bread with *posca*, water mixed with sour wine or vinegar and flavored with herbs. Posca would hydrate them, while making them just a little bit drunk (to put up with long hours and dreadful conditions?). Herbs made the taste tolerable, and the acidity killed harmful bacteria. Posca contained vitamin C and helped prevent scurvy, which resulted in weakness and anemia. Did posca prolong the lives of miners and increase slave owner profits by postponing the cost of replacing slaves? Could be. The rich got richer.

Slaves excavated mine shafts roughly six-feet square and as deep as one hundred feet. They dug shafts in stages, searching for ore veins. When ore was found, slaves chipped away for days at the ore-bearing rock with iron chisels, hammers, and picks, creating tunnels or narrow, low galleries that followed the veins horizontally. Unexcavated stone supported the tunnel roof.

Many shaft walls offered hand- and footholds, also niches to place oil lamps; others had holes in the sides in which pieces of wood could be inserted, forming ladders. Poor ventilation was a common hazard, as well as overseers who forced slaves to work harder until they collapsed. Remember, they were only replaceable parts in an economic system. The majority of slaves were privately owned, while state-owned slaves made up the remainder. Regardless of who owned them, the miners labored on the bottom rung of Athens's slavery ladder, holding on for dear life and relaxing their grip only in death.

Farms. Agricultural slaves obviously lived and worked in a much more favorable environment than the miners. Although they sweated profusely in summer's heat for rich landowners, at least they were able to breathe fresh air. These large landowners required an endless supply of slaves to till the soil, plant seeds, weed the rows, water, and harvest various crops. Farms grew grains and vegetables, including barley, wheat, millet, cabbage, onions, garlic, lentils, chickpeas, and beans. Orchards produced figs, olives, almonds, and pomegranates; vineyards hung heavy with grapes. Familiar herbs such as thyme, savory, sage, oregano, and mint needed weeding and cultivation. Farm slaves also fed and watered animals, including goats, sheep, pigs, chickens, geese, oxen, mules, cattle, donkeys, and horses. The work never ended.

Although the area surrounding Athens encompassed numerous small farms, very few of these farms had slaves; farmers couldn't afford to buy them and feed them. Instead, the farm family took care of its own property.

Households. Further up the ladder, domestic slaves, primarily women, worked as nurses, playmates, teachers, housekeepers, and stewards—washing, spinning, weaving, cooking, and serving meals. They did household chores such as preparing the bath and bedchambers

(Greek custom permitted the master to rape his slaves). The domestic slaves integrated themselves more easily into family life and enjoyed more comfort and security than other kinds of slaves. However, the wise ones never assumed too much, because their position in the household still depended upon the whim of their masters. These domestics comprised one of the largest categories of Athenian slaves.

Workshops. Artisan slaves occupied the rung above the domestics. They offered creative, managerial, and manufacturing skills to numerous small businesses and commercial workshops. These slaves designed, crafted, and produced goods such as clothes, sandals, knives, shields, couches, lamps, pottery, and so on. They often worked with contractors on public buildings by sculpting stone and applying decorative paint.

Private slave owners rented their artisan slaves to small and large workshops on a daily basis. Owning a stable of slaves for hire provided a good living for the slave owner and a relatively independent life for the slave. In many cases the artisan slave lived outside the master's household, found a place of employment, sometimes formed a family, and earned a small wage, despite his slave status.

Services. On the top rung of the Athenian slavery ladder were educated slaves who lived and worked, often independently, in return for wages, food, and clothing. Private slaves ranged from menial laborers to managers, accountants to bankers, and dealers to doctors; public slaves included street sweepers, inspectors of weights and measures, scribes, police, and even executioners. Many public slaves became skillful civil servants whom the state relied on to carry out day-to-day governmental duties. The public slaves of Athens knew tradition, policies, and procedures for getting things done. These civil servants may have helped prepare the way for manumission (i.e., the formal release from bondage by a slave's master). The money they earned and saved enabled some of them to buy their freedom.

Status and Population of Slaves

Despite the favored work environment that the workshops and services slaves enjoyed, they still were not free. Their owners considered them as furniture or livestock that could be bought and sold. They were treated as beasts of burden that produced goods and services at a profit for their masters.

Owners did just about anything with slaves that they wanted to: they beat, flogged, raped, rented, and sold them. They replaced the native language of their slaves with Greek and usually renamed them. These names appeared on no official city-state register except for inventories of possessions. Although slaves were viewed generally as nonpersons, without them the healthy economic life of Athens would have slowed to a crawl.

Some statistics in ancient texts have overstated the number of slaves in Athens during its golden age in the fifth century BC. Many historians, however, believe there were roughly 70,000 slaves or 45 percent of the total population of 155,000. That's a lot of predominantly white slaves who looked like their owners. Some slaves might have thought how easy it would be to escape or rebel and mingle among the general population. But very few did, when compared with the servile (slave) rebellions against Rome in the next chapter.

In the preface to this section, I quoted British historian Keith Hopkins as saying that when slaves numbered at least 20 percent of the population and played an important part in the production of goods and services, then *that* society was a slave society. Based on his point of view, the city-state of ancient Athens may have been history's first slave society as well as the progenitor of modern slavery known as human trafficking.

Now, let's take a look at imperial Rome.

CHAPTER 2

Imperial Rome: The Most Brutal Slave Society of Its Time

During imperial times, the slave markets of Rome were the largest and busiest in the world, selling not only captured soldiers, but men, women, and children from every corner of the vast Roman Empire.

RICHARD WATKINS,
SLAVERY BONDAGE THROUGHOUT HISTORY

EXPERT USE OF STATE TERROR

FOR A THOUSAND YEARS, ROMAN armies left more bodies littered around the landscape or crucified on crosses than any other society. For example, Roman legionnaires pursued an army of former slaves led by Spartacus, losing battle after battle to his forces for over two years. In 71 BC the Roman army finally cornered and defeated him. Spartacus died on the battlefield while six thousand of his soldiers were captured.

Marcus Licinius Crassus, the victorious general, condemned these rebels to death. They were crucified and displayed on a 200-kilometer (124-mile) section of the Appian Way from Rome to Capua. That's a crucified slave every 110 feet for 124 miles.

Dying slowly of exposure or asphyxiation and then rotting away, these slaves remained on view for weeks so travelers could ponder the fate of anyone who dared to rebel against the Roman state. Imagine the slaves' suffering, their cries and then silence, the stench, and vultures tearing at flesh. Death by crucifixion punished slaves, pirates, the worst of criminals, enemies of the state, and the lower classes. Members of Roman society, however, were rarely subject to capital punishment, except for high treason; instead they were fined or exiled.

Specialized military teams, consisting of a centurion and four soldiers, crucified each victim on a vertical pole (*crux simplex*), a wooden T (*crux commissa*), or a cross (*crux immissa*). The more people these teams crucified, the more efficient they became at arranging arms and legs on the poles and crosses and knowing where to place the five- to seven-inch iron nails or spikes in the victim's body. Sometimes soldiers broke the victim's legs with an iron bar to increase pain and hasten death, which could take from a few hours to a few days.

Weeks afterward, the nails were often extracted and reused.

Constantine the Great, the first Christian emperor, abolished crucifixion throughout the Roman Empire in AD 337 out of veneration of Jesus Christ.

How Rome Was Founded

Mars and Murder gave birth to Rome in 753 BC. Legend claimed that Mars, the god of war, fathered Romulus and Remus. These twin brothers had agreed to build a city, and yet they disagreed over which brother would rule it and what to call it. Romulus settled the dispute by killing

Remus and then named the city Rome, after himself. He became the city's first king, the commander-in-chief of the army, the chief judicial authority, and the initiator of Roman slavery.

Seven different kings, including Romulus, ruled the Roman Kingdom from 753 to 509 BC (244 years). The Roman Republic succeeded the kingdom from 509 to 27 BC (482 years). The republic was then replaced by the Roman Empire from 27 BC to AD 476 (503 years). Rome dominated its part of the world for more than 1,200 years based on two fundamental factors: *military success* and *slavery*. Successful military campaigns enslaved an estimated three million people, who produced, sustained, and prolonged the fluctuating economic health of the Roman state, regardless of its form of government.

Beginning of Roman Slavery

According to Dionysius, of Halicarnassus, an ancient teacher and historian, Romulus initiated Roman slavery by giving fathers the right to sell their own children as slaves. Once this door opened, the usual slave-gathering practices of war, kidnapping, piracy, birth, debt, and crime muscled their way through the doorway. During the first two decades of the Roman Kingdom, Romulus waged several local wars that added to Rome's territories, population, and number of slaves. Then for many hundreds of years, soldiers of the Roman Kingdom, Republic, and Empire marched in all directions around the Mediterranean Sea and into Gaul and Britain. They captured, chained, and forwarded an increasing number of slaves in one direction…toward Rome.

Rome: the seat of power. Rome: the center of an empire of 55 million people during the life of Christ. Rome: the world's largest appetite for food, olive oil, wine, cruelty, and slaves. Rome: the winner of continuous warfare and its booty of riches at the expense of conquered territories. Rome: the forum for brilliant administrators, superior engineers, hardened soldiers, corrupt politicians, and wealthy aristocrats, also known as patricians. Rome: the most enduring slave society of its time.

Expansion of Roman Slavery

Along with most goods and services, the spread of slavery paralleled the expansion and contraction of the Roman economy. The number of slaves increased when money was plentiful and decreased when money was scarce. Five major components shaped the economy of the Roman Kingdom: military success, agriculture, industry, trade, and slavery. Military victories produced an increasing number of slaves who farmed large estates or toiled in mines, small-scale industries, and villas. Military losses (resulting in no captives) reduced the supply of slaves and provided fewer goods and services for the people.

The economy ebbed and flowed from the Roman Kingdom to about halfway through the Roman Republic in 270 BC. During this period wealthy landowners enlarged their holdings at the expense of small farmers and peasants. The rich foreclosed properties when smaller owners became debtors or seized other properties by use of force or political influence. Despite the sizable accumulative resources of patricians, Rome's economic health was periodically unstable for about five hundred years.

Then in 264 BC, Rome's fortunes began to change. For the next two hundred years, numerous successful wars generated one of the largest transfers of wealth in the history of the world from conquered people to victorious Rome. Booty flowed into Rome year after year, decade after decade, and beyond. As money poured into Rome's treasury, the city cancelled taxes for its citizens while increasing taxes on the rest of its expanding empire. Military successes generated an enormous amount of gold, vast stores of precious gems, a limitless number of possessions, innumerable domestic animals, numerous wild beasts for use in gladiatorial arenas, and an unending supply of slaves.

An influx of hundreds of thousands of new slaves, many to replace those who wore out and died, continued decade after decade for two centuries. Predominantly white, they came from around the Mediterranean and all parts of Europe. Some black slaves, mostly from central Africa, also became captives of the Romans. By 50 BC an estimated one million slaves labored on large farms and orchards in fertile areas of the Italian peninsula. Many thousands toiled under dark, dank, deadly conditions in Spanish silver mines. Tens of thousands of slaves worked in Rome's households, artisan workshops, and public institutions. A few thousand fought in gladiatorial contests (where many died) or rowed in galleys with free men during labor shortages. By AD 14 the aggregate number of Roman slaves, past and present, numbered three million. They produced profits for a myriad number of landowners and businesses throughout the peninsula and the far-flung empire for several centuries.

Slaves accounted for 25 percent of Rome's one million city residents. To keep track of these mostly white slaves, who mingled easily among Rome's citizenry, a proposal surfaced in the Roman senate that would require all slaves to wear uniform clothing for easy identification. Those in favor of this idea felt that uniform clothing would help to prevent slaves from fleeing from their masters; they could be readily recognized and returned. Other senators argued that uniform clothing would focus attention on how many slaves there were in Rome, about one-fourth of the population! After much debate the proposal was voted down, perhaps because the government feared an uprising. Three slave wars in the last 150 years may have fed this fear.

Treatment of Roman Slaves

The Romans became expert abusers of slaves. They flogged, bludgeoned, branded, chained, starved, imprisoned, raped, or killed their slaves for real or imagined offenses. Originally, Roman law during the kingdom, republic, and early years of the empire protected the master whether or not a reason existed. However, as the empire aged, laws became more humane, although slaves were still considered property and could be mistreated.

Consider this incident: When a clumsy slave boy broke a crystal cup, his enraged master grabbed him and started to throw the lad into a pool that held several large eel-like lampreys. This jawless fish has a funnel-shaped, sucking mouth of horny teeth; it usually attaches itself to the side of a larger fish, bores a hole in the fish, and sucks out its blood. Would the lampreys do this with a child? The boy begged and received mercy from an important visitor to his master's house. The visitor became angry with the slave owner over this proposed punishment and ordered that *all* of the owner's crystal cups be smashed. Seneca the Younger described this incident in *De Ira*, a treatise on the consequences of anger. The slave owner was Vedius Pollio; the compassionate visitor was Emperor Augustus!

Although a master could kill a slave and go unpunished, of course, the reverse was not the same. According to Roman law, if a slave killed his master, not only would the slave be tortured and executed, but also all of the other slaves in the household could be, too. Tacitus, a Roman senator and historian, noted that the Senate debated an incident of this type in AD 61. Some senators pointed out that not enforcing the law would invite rebellion. Since slaves greatly outnumbered the master and his staff, the state (on behalf of the dead master) should intervene and exercise control. The law must be followed. This argument prevailed. The guilty slave and many innocent household slaves, including women and children, were tortured and executed.

THREE SERVILE (SLAVE) REBELLIONS

Although the first of three major slave wars erupted around 135 BC on Sicily, its causes can be traced to a time many decades earlier in the middle of Rome's Second Punic War with Carthage. (The site of this ancient city is near Tunis in North Africa today.) While the war raged on, Roman speculators hurried to Sicily and purchased land at low prices. They also occupied estates that had been forfeited to Rome after the pro-Carthage owners fled or were executed. Those favoring Rome became rich, while common citizens without influence descended deeper into poverty.

As the number of peasants and slaves increased, the gap between the poor and wealthy grew larger. During this period, Sicily prospered as slaves planted and harvested grain on large farms. In addition, they cultivated olives and grapes for consumption in Rome. Abundant food, destined for patricians, was withheld from impoverished Sicilian peasants and slaves. Civil unrest simmered on this island, once regarded as paradise.

A sizable number of slaves on Sicily had been enemy soldiers. At one time they had marched with heads held high, shields firmly fixed on one arm with a sword in the other hand, eager to throw themselves against Roman troops. Now in chains they trudged behind a plow, planted, hoed, harvested, or drove slow-moving ox carts. These former warriors shared the same status as the oxen: a possession of someone else. Chances are their slave owners had never risked their lives in war. The slave-warriors may have thought, how much longer will we live like this? Is rebellion the answer? Maybe, but any attempt was punished by crucifixion. The threat of a painful and slow, excruciating death kept slaves sullen but not rebellious.

Since Sicily was only a stone's throw across the Strait of Messina from mainland Italy, numerous runaway slaves fled to this island. The Sicilian mountains provided many places to hide and plan an uprising. But who would lead it? Who would meld together the runaways, the agricultural slave-warriors, and the other slaves? In the town of Enna in the center of Sicily, the answer was slowly forming.

Eunus, a charismatic Syrian household slave, would lead the **First Servile War**. He was a fortune-teller and a magician, a spinner of prophecies, and the leader of an underground organization. In 135 BC Eunus seized the town of Enna with four hundred slaves, and they did ugly things by murdering slave owners, raping women, and killing children. Within a few days, they freed thousands of agricultural slaves, and their numbers grew from four hundred to six thousand and then to ten thousand. Eunus changed his name to King Antiochus, a royal Syrian name, and led his slave army to victory against eight thousand Sicilian troops. He envisioned conquering Sicily and turning it into an island ruled by slaves.

Rome had other ideas, although it took three years to perfect them. In 132 BC a Roman commander named Piso landed on Sicily and attacked the city of Morgantina, killing eight thousand defenders and crucifying others. Piso then seized several cities including Enna, where he killed and crucified even more slaves. King Antiochus fled to the hills, was captured, and, oddly enough, was not crucified by the Roman army. He died in prison. Thousands of his slave-warriors, who refused to live as farm animals, suffered the painful death they had feared. To avoid crucifixion, some committed suicide.

The **Second Servile War** lasted from 104 BC until 100 BC. Begun and fought in Sicily, it attracted thousands of slaves. At one point the rebel army of 20,000 infantry and 2,000 cavalry controlled almost all of Sicily. After three years of fierce fighting under several different commanders, Rome finally prevailed. Fewer than a thousand slaves survived. They were taken to Rome to fight in the gladiatorial arenas, where they were killed by wild beasts or by their comrades, according to a mutual agreement. Then the last one standing committed suicide.

The **Third Servile War,** described at the beginning of this chapter, was led by Spartacus and lasted from 73 BC to 71 BC. It, too, ended in defeat by the Roman legionnaires.

Each servile rebellion began because thousands of slaves decided that enough was enough. Their lives of dull servitude or endless labor prodded them to risk death in order to escape the chains of slavery. They fought, lost inevitably, and died.

Decline of Roman Slavery

For centuries slavery filled an indispensable financial need in Rome's economy. Without unpaid slave labor, wealthy landowners would have realized lower profits and the state would have built fewer public buildings. Also, Rome's government would not have functioned as smoothly as it did without the contribution of educated public slaves who became gifted civil servants. As the pace of Rome's conquests slowed in the second century AD, there were fewer slaves available for agriculture and industry. For decades, tens of thousands of slaves and a smaller number of free men had labored together. Now a shortage of slaves opened up opportunities for free men, many of whom became tenant farmers. Over time these tenants reluctantly accepted the beginning stages of serfdom or risked being replaced by others who agreed to be bound to the soil as serfs. This new form of farming prepared the way a few centuries later for medieval European serfdom, considered by many as a new form of slavery.

The Roman Empire had not yet abolished slavery as it entered the third century AD, even though emperor after emperor introduced more humane legislation: laws that protected slave owners were modified to protect slaves; slave trading became a shunned business; fathers could no longer sell children; and slave hunters, instead of fugitive slaves, could be executed. Rome's slave-based economy slowly eroded as manumission (freeing of slaves) increased.

By 230 the Franks, the Goths, and the Visigoths had invaded the empire in Spain, Gaul, and provinces that the Danube River flowed through. As these intruders overran the borders, slaves and peasants fled farms and orchards. Others helped build walls around panicked cities. Roman commanders of different field armies fought the invaders with varying results. When the invaders won, they sold the defeated Roman soldiers to slave dealers, who found buyers within the empire. Once again some Romans made a lot of money by buying and selling their countrymen. During this period slavery revived and then declined, but it never completely disappeared. Slavery was too established as a profitable business within Roman society.

End of the Roman Empire

Rome held center stage in its part of the world for more than twelve hundred years, an extraordinary performance. It was only a matter of time, however, until numerous wars along Rome's lengthy borders created administrative and defensive problems; the empire had grown too large and was stretched too thin to adequately protect its citizens. Therefore, Emperor Diocletian divided the empire into western and eastern regions in 285. He felt this would help the military become more nimble and successful in responding to aggressors.

Diocletian ruled the eastern region from Byzantium (renamed Constantinople in 330). Another emperor governed the western region from Rome. During the next 150 years or so under various emperors, the Roman Empire was reunited and divided three more times. As slavery declined and military enlistments decreased, the western region became exposed to savage adversaries who were more brutal than Rome. The recognized end of the Western Roman Empire occurred in 476. That's when Flavius Odoacer deposed Emperor Romulus Augustulus, divided the empire into several kingdoms, and engaged in many tribal wars.

The fall of Rome created a power vacuum in Europe and around the Mediterranean Basin at the beginning of the Middle Ages. This vacuum was gradually filled during the next several centuries by two conflicting theologies—Christianity (decreed in 380 as the state religion of the Roman Empire) and Islam (begun in 622)—*plus* the infighting of numerous warlords. These "warlords" included kings, queens, princes, princesses, caliphs, sultans, sheiks, khans, and leaders of various ethnic groups scattered throughout Europe, North Africa, and Asia. From the fifth century to the fifteenth century, these leaders and their followers were extremely busy plundering, torturing, raping, killing, and enslaving hundreds of thousands of common people as well as those with power and influence.

The Eastern Roman Empire, also known as the Byzantine Empire, survived until 1453. After a two-month siege of Constantinople, the Ottoman Turks prevailed, eradicating the lingering vestiges of the Roman Empire. This history-changing event slowed the flow of white slaves from areas around the Black Sea into European states lining the northern shore of the Mediterranean Sea. To fill this labor shortage, trans-Saharan caravans, controlled by Arabs, brought black captives from Central Africa to North African ports, where slave ships waited.

CONCLUSION
Times Change; Slavery Doesn't

Now that you have visited two significant societies of the ancient world, do you think that slavery ended when the Eastern Roman Empire died? Not a chance. The business of buying and selling people—a forerunner of human trafficking—was too lucrative. African kings, Arab slavers, European invaders, and American businessmen, each driven by the profit motive, eagerly captured and sold (greed) black Africans around the world for unpaid work (slavery) and coerced sex (rape).

You'll find more in Part Two: Black Slaves of the New World.

PART TWO
Black Slaves of the New World

PREFACE
Random Hazards of History

IMAGINE YOU ARE LIVING TWO hundred, four hundred, or even six hundred years ago in Africa. Several men creep into your village in the middle of the night. The intruders enter your hut wielding daggers, swords, and rifles and carrying ropes, handcuffs, and leg and neck irons. You hear sounds, shrieks, scuffles. The intruders overpower your father and mother, seize your brother and sister. They look for others and find you.

All family members are swiftly bound, manacled. You stumble outside into darkness. Yoked together, you walk farther this night and the next day and the next week than you have ever walked before. You fear you will never see your home again.

Swarthy Arab slavers force you across the burning Sahara Desert to ports in North Africa or brothels in Cairo. Maybe you are taken to boats in Zanzibar bound for the fleshpots of the Orient. Or raiding tribesmen herd you and dozens of captives to Ouidah, a port on the west coast of Africa. You will be held at a slave site—Portuguese, English, French, Dutch, or Danish—until the captain of a trans-Atlantic slave ship is ready to sail, eager to have you aboard as his cargo. In any case, you are torn from your family, alone at age eight or fifteen with strangers. You are afraid, terrified, crying. If you cry too much, you could be killed with the quick thrust of a sword to your belly.

You have been kidnapped. Next month you will be auctioned.

K. G. Richardson

Once you are sold to someone, somewhere, you will start your life over as a slave, owned by another person in the same way as a dog or an ox. Your master will change your name, dictate your labor, and try to reshape your thoughts. He will rape your body and crush your spirit. You will obey him and his cruel overseers, or your flesh may be torn apart with repeated whippings. Some slaves will resist; most will not.

What would you have done?

CHAPTER 3

The Enslavers: Africans, Arabs, Europeans, and Americans

AFRICA PLUNDERED

MORE THAN TWO THOUSAND YEARS ago, black Africans sought to enslave each other as numerous tribal groups competed to create regional kingdoms. Century after century these groups perpetuated slavery based on some of the same reasons used by Athens and Rome (i.e., war, debt, kidnapping, and crime). In addition, the forced exchange of family members for food occurred during periods of famine. Some of these tribes made the seemingly humane offer of buying orphans and unwanted children as slaves. If they had not made this offer, children might have been abandoned and left to die. Although the black owners and black slave children usually did not share the same tribal bloodline, these newly purchased dependents could eventually become members of their owners' family. Ironically, this possibility provided the young slaves with a sense of kinship, giving them a personal identity as well as a greater ability to survive in a dangerous world.

As the centuries unfolded, external forces would slowly erode any "family-oriented" form of slavery and replace it with the more common and harsher master/slave relationship. These types of owners considered slaves to be property and offered them little opportunity to improve their status. Other, more warlike, African states enslaved black captives for their own use or traded them for money with three kinds of foreigners—Arabs, Europeans, and Americans—who sent slaves to many parts of the world using caravan and water routes.

Arabs dominated several of these well-traveled routes, including the trans-Saharan Desert, Red Sea, and the Indian Ocean (or East African) passage to Persia, India, and China. Major westward routes shipped slaves from West *and* East African ports across the Atlantic Ocean to North, Central, and South America, and to several Caribbean islands. Other routes sent slaves north to Europe.

Elikia M'Bokolo, renowned historian of the Democratic Republic of Congo, expounded on the slave routes in an April 1998 article in *Le Monde diplomatique*, an international newspaper: "The African continent was bled of its human resources via all possible routes. Across the Sahara, through the Red Sea, from the Indian Ocean ports and across the Atlantic. At least ten centuries of slavery for the benefit of the Muslim countries (from the ninth to the nineteenth)."

He continued: "Four million slaves exported via the Red Sea, another four million through the Swahili ports of the Indian Ocean, perhaps as many as nine million along the trans-Saharan caravan route, and eleven to twenty million (depending on the author) across the Atlantic Ocean." Based on his estimates, the slaves on these arduous journeys numbered a minimum of twenty-eight million and a maximum of thirty-seven million.

Patrick Manning, in his book *Slavery and African Life,* pointed out that for every two slaves exported from Africa, one remained. These slaves served kings, tribes, governments, societies, empires, businesses, and individual owners inside Africa. Using Mr. M'Bokolo's minimum estimate of *twenty-eight million slaves*, it is possible *fourteen million* slaves were left behind *within* Africa. These two estimates add up to *forty-two million slaves*––chained, flogged, raped, faced with despair, deprived of family and future—casualties of a profit-driven economic system known today as human trafficking.

Historic henchmen of HT are among the following:

AFRICANS: Kings, Tribes, Traders, Raiders

Mansa Musa I, King of Mali from 1312 to 1327. Musa lucked out by being in the right place at the right time. Here's how: the king who preceded him sent an expedition of two hundred boats to explore the extent of the Atlantic Ocean. He ordered the captain *not* to return until the crew's food and water was gone or until they found out where the ocean ended. After a long time, only the captain's boat returned. He said the other boats were sucked into a huge whirlpool. The king did not believe him and became determined to explore the ocean himself. This time the king ordered two thousand boats for himself and his men and one thousand boats for food and water. He appointed Musa as king in his absence. After an entire year no one returned, no one was heard from, and Mansa Musa, the interim ruler, became Mali's new king. (*Mansa* means king; *Musa* means Moses, his name.)

The Mali Empire contained valuable natural resources—gold, salt, copper—and enjoyed an excellent location in West Africa. Trans-Saharan caravans arrived and left from Timbuktu, one of Mali's major cities. This site near the Upper Niger River also provided easy transit from the interior to the Atlantic Ocean. These land and water routes gave Mali access to markets for many products, including slaves.

(Note: As in ancient Athens and imperial Rome, slaves were an essential part of Mali's social and economic life. They worked in fields and homes, held administrative posts, served in the army, and were bought, sold, and bartered just like any other product. Slavery is still a very profitable business in Mali with thousands of people enslaved.)

Musa, a Muslim black African, knew that at some point he would make a pilgrimage to Mecca about four thousand miles away. When he made this journey in 1324–25, his entourage included twelve thousand slaves, five hundred of which preceded him, each carrying a four-pound staff of gold. Eighty camels walked behind each laden with a three-hundred-pound bag of gold dust. Musa spent and gave away so much gold in Cairo on his way to Mecca that he inadvertently depreciated the value of gold in the Middle East for a decade. Inflation occurred, and it cost everyone more money to buy products and services.

Although Musa was believed to have been the richest man in the world at that time (some claim *today* that he was the richest man in the history of the world!), he ran out of money on the pilgrimage and had to borrow funds for his journey home. Once home he could easily repay the loan, since Mali had three large gold mines inside of its border. And, guess what? Mali's king controlled the output. As word of Mali's wealth reached the Mediterranean Basin and southern Europe, merchants from Venice, Genoa, and Granada started to include Timbuktu in their travel plans. They were eager to trade goods for gold and slaves.

Many Muslim artisans and scholars returned from Mecca with Musa to Timbuktu. They helped him transform this trans-Saharan trading post into a cultural, intellectual, and spiritual center. In addition to mosques, they built a library that eventually held one of the world's greatest collections of ancient manuscripts—astronomy, mathematics, law, medicine, and the teachings of Islam from the thirteenth to the sixteenth centuries. Today Timbuktu (aka Tombouctou) is a UNESCO World Heritage Site.

Kingdom of Dahomey, "The Slave Coast," West Africa. From 1600 to 1900, Dahomey (known today as Benin) participated in exporting up to 20 percent of all slaves sent to Europe and the Americas via Dutch, British, French, and Portuguese merchant ships. Under King

Agaja, who ruled from 1708 to 1740, Dahomey became a regional power in the 1720s by conquering nearby city-states, as various tribes struggled for area dominance in the slave trade. He defeated Allada in 1724 and Whydah (aka Ouidah) in 1727–28, gaining access to the Atlantic Ocean for landlocked Dahomey and making it a major trader on the Bight (Bay) of Benin. In a few years, Agaja doubled the territory of Dahomey and increased its capability to process more slaves, resulting in more profits.

After Agaja conquered Allada, he sent tribute (part of the booty) to the Oyo Empire. (Dahomey had been a vassal state of the Oyos since the 1680s.) However, the Oyo king thought he should have received more money from Agaja. To express his displeasure, the Oyo king sent his army to burn down Abomey, a major city in Dahomey. This initiated warfare that lasted several years, weakening Dahomey and making it vulnerable to other tribes. To have his army appear stronger, Agaja dressed hundreds of women in battle garb and placed them in the back ranks of the army to increase its size. This ruse worked so well that an opposing army fled. On other days when fighting flared, the women fought bravely and effectively, qualifying them as a special regiment in the army. In awe of their prowess, some European observers compared the women to that mythical race of female warriors known as Amazons.

Seventy years later, King Gezo of Dahomey, who ruled from 1818 to 1858, waged annual wars and sold captives into slavery, which increased revenue, reduced taxes, and enabled him to purchase firearms. In addition to his male army, he relied upon four thousand of the battle-tested Amazons, whose future members were recruited from war captives and free Dahomians, some as young as eight years old. Rigorous training honed aggressiveness as they learned to fight with sabers and guns.

Dahomey participated in the slave trade to improve its economy since other products, such as palm oil, agriculture, and crafts, generated insufficient funds. The Dahomians became so successful as slave raiders and traders that the West African coast was referred to as "The Slave Coast" by European and New World merchants. It was dotted with several ports that exported slaves supplied by various African kingdoms, empires, and tribes. This section of coast sent some two million slaves on their way to an inhumane passage and unknown future on the other side of the Atlantic Ocean; many died en route. A smaller number of slaves were shipped to England, Portugal, and Spain.

The Imbangala Marauders, West Central Africa. About one thousand miles south of Ouidah on the West Central African coast are several former slave seaports—Ambriz, Benguela, Cabinda, Kilongo, Loango, Luanda, Malemba, and Mayumba. Established by the Portuguese over several decades, the ports were scattered along four hundred miles of coastline. From 1500 to 1900, these embarkation points shipped twice as many slaves as the Slave Coast ports north of them. Most of these four million slaves ended up working on plantations in Brazil and on Caribbean Islands.

Raiders and traders in West Central Africa seized a large number of natives in Angola, Kongo, and adjacent territories during the sixteen and seventeen hundreds. Continuous warfare over these potential slaves involved empires and tribes, including kingdoms of Kongo, Matamba, and Ndongo. In addition, nomadic marauders, known as the Imbangala, pillaged and plundered the area in pursuit of slaves. Some historians think this group may have originated in Central Africa and migrated southward to Angola around 1600. Or, perhaps they were local people of southern Angola from the Bihe Plateau or coastal regions west of the highlands and south of the Kwanza River. No one knows for sure.

The Imbangala founded a militaristic society that rejected farming, cattle ranching, and a kinship lifestyle. Instead, they perfected warlike capabilities that permitted them to seize land, crops, and cattle for their own use. After they ravaged an area, they moved on to take land and food from someone else. To subdue their victims, the Imbangala used familiar weapons—bows and arrows, swords, knives—plus war clubs or hatchets in maniacal hand-to-hand combat that produced panic among their prey. When they wanted something, they just took it, usually violently.

Most of the opponents of the Imbangala had received little military training and defended themselves with common hunting weapons. These natives lacked the intensive exercise and strict discipline of the Imbangala, who practiced daily and improved their skills in mock battles and armed war dances, enacting offensive and defensive moves.

Their reputation as cannibals preceded the Imbangala, causing many adversaries to flee when they heard the Imbangala were coming. Initiation into this cult included being taught torture, human sacrifice, and cannibalism. Recruits could not become members until they had made their first kill. Then they ate fallen enemy soldiers, drank palm tree alcohol, and prepared themselves for the next battle.

The Imbangala and other ruthless groups fought to supply slaves to the Portuguese in return for guns. These competitors also tried to exterminate each other. Early in the seventeenth century, some Imbangala members decided to leave the tribe maybe realizing their lifestyle could be a lose-lose situation. In 1620 they founded a new kingdom named Kasanje (after their leader), ceased marauding, survived, and yet *retained* the name Imbangala—to intimidate others? Old habits are hard to break.

ARABS: SLAVE TRADER, SULTAN, CALIPH

Tippu Tip, Slave Trader. He was born on Zanzibar in 1837 of a Swahili father and Arabian mother. Tippu Tip (a future nickname) was really named Hamed bin Muhammed, which is spelled in various ways, depending upon the historian. Also, there are differing explanations for the origin of his nickname: he had a nervous twitch affecting his eyes; he was named after a local bird, called Tippu Tib, that blinked a lot; or the guns of his Arab slavers made the sound tip-pu-tip.

Regardless of his nickname, this trader in ivory and slaves terrorized Central Africa from the east coast to the interior. Some sources considered him the most powerful slaver in Africa. To get ivory, he killed or enslaved the natives who hunted the elephants. Tip often negotiated low prices for ivory, usually under depredating conditions—he torched villages at dawn and shot many natives as they tried to escape the flames. Survivors eagerly agreed to his terms.

Other times, he captured everyone he could get his hands on, as long as they generated income (i.e., pretty girls wrapped in colorful clothing for sale as sex slaves or healthy young boys with smooth skin who were sold for the same reason). Regardless of the product, regardless of its purpose, Tip pursued a successful continuation of the slave business started by his grandfather and inherited by his father; at age eighteen he was working hard to outdo his dad.

By the 1880s, Tip had accumulated wealth, power, and contacts with many famous men, such as David Livingstone, a Scottish missionary and physician, and Henry Morton Stanley, a Welsh journalist and explorer. He arranged escorts for them to the African interior, as well as helping them plan routes and acquire supplies. "In return, the white men liked him and were impressed with his wealth, power, intelligence, ambition, and cruelty," Leda Farrant reported in her book titled *Tippu Tip and the East African Slave Trade*, 1975.

(Note: it seems odd that these two admired men of the Western world would be impressed with Tip's "cruelty.")

As slave trading, illegal for decades, dwindled away in the 1890s, Tip retreated to Zanzibar, where he owned seven clove plantations and ten thousand slaves. Reportedly, he "visited" the sex slaves in his harem twice a day. He died June 14, 1905.

Moulay Ismail, Sultan of Morocco. Meet one of history's poster boys of slavery and rape, as well as torture and death. During his fifty-five-year reign, from 1672 to 1727, he acquired the nickname "The Bloodthirsty" for obvious reasons:

1. During his first year in power, Ismail displayed in the city of Fez some four hundred heads of slain enemies.
2. If men (other than approved eunuchs) looked at his wives or sex slaves, the men were killed, usually beheaded.
3. During his fifty-five years of despotism, he tortured and killed thirty thousand people in addition to those who died in battle.

Among his "people" possessions, Ismail had a slave army of 150,000 men from sub-Saharan Africa known as the Black Guard. Also, twenty-five thousand kidnapped and pirated slaves, mostly European Christians, who labored under harsh conditions to build a palace that would rival King Louis XIV's Palace of Versailles in France. And a harem of five hundred sex slaves; some sources indicated two thousand.

(Note: The harems of pre-Islamic and Muslim Arabs were status symbols; the more power and wealth the potentate possessed, the more non-Muslim women he captured, enslaved, and raped. These women were in bondage for one reason—to serve as vessels for their slave owners' ejaculate. When they gave birth, they were offered a choice—convert to Islam or die, usually by beheading. Who knows how many brave, devout non-Muslim mothers chose death? Then, the Muslim woman appointed to raise the baby became its "mother." How many children grew up without wondering why they had fair skin and blue eyes?)

Based on a few estimates, Ismail sired from 1,042 to 1,171 children. The lower estimate is according to the *Guinness Book of World Records*, and the higher estimate is from reports by a diplomat, Dominique Busnot, who traveled to Morocco for the French monarchy. The two kingdoms had a business relationship and a common interest—they each trafficked in slaves.

Within the past few years, two anthropologists from the University of Vienna, Austria, wondered whether Ismail could really have begotten so many children. How often would he have had sexual intercourse with different slaves to achieve this result? They developed a computer program to find out. After inputting many variables, it appeared that if Ismail had had sex at least once a day for thirty-two years, the answer was *probably yes*. And this was with a hypothetical harem of 65 to 110 women; instead, Ismail had 500 to 2,000 slaves available to rape. Once a day? Twice? More?

Their findings were published in the February 14, 2014, issue of the journal *PLOS ONE*. The curious researchers/authors are Elisabeth Oberzaucher and Karl Grammer. Their study is titled *The Case of Moulay Ismael--Fact or Fancy?* They designed a thorough approach and wrote an informative report. (You may notice there's a slight difference in the spelling of Moulay's last name.)

Moulay was born in 1645 and gained the throne in 1672 when his brother, the sultan, was thrown from a horse and died. Within several years, Ismail brutally consolidated a sprawling country beset with tribal factions. Then he successfully fought the Ottoman Turks three times—in 1679, 1682, and 1695/96—to maintain Morocco's independence. These victories earned him the title of "Warrior King."

At age eighty-two, this feared sultan had become a doddering, drooling, nearly toothless shell of a man, spitting up sputum into a handkerchief held by a slave who followed him around for that sole purpose. Ismail died in 1727 of natural causes. A violent death would have been more fitting.

Abd-ar-Rahman III, Caliph of Cordoba. His fifty-year reign in Spain (912–962) featured jealousy, murder, miscegenation, war, and sex. The cast of characters included his mother, a Christian sex slave; his father, the assassinated son of the emir; one of his uncles, the assassin; his Muslim Arab grandfather, the emir (who ordered the murder of his own son!); and numerous extras representing warring Muslim, Arab, and Christian factions that Abd-ar-Rahman fought with and against decade after decade in various parts of Islamic Spain.

SYNOPSIS: The Beginning

Abd-ar-Rahman III is twenty-one years old. His dying grandfather, the emir, appoints the grandson as his successor and gives Abd-ar-Rahman his ring, the symbol of power. The emir dies on October 15 in 912, and Abd-ar-Rahman assumes leadership of the emirate. Although the transition is apparently smooth, several dangers await the young, untested ruler:

[Enter Chaos.]

- The emirate he inherits is in disarray as groups challenge his ability to rule. He responds within ten days by exhibiting the head of a local rebel leader.
- Islamic Spain (aka Al-Andalus) is shrinking and becoming less powerful as Christians fight (in a struggle known as the *Reconquista*) to regain territory taken by the Muslims, beginning in 711.
- Two warring factions within the emirate add to widespread unrest: the Muladi, a centuries-old dominant population of mixed ancestry (Muslim men and non-Muslim women), are considered "inferior" by newly arrived Arab aristocrats because of "religious intermingling." However, since the Muladi were first in Al-Andalus, they feel the aristocrats are invaders. Infighting erupts, frequently.

From Emir to Caliph

The above are just a few of the concerns facing Abd-ar-Rahman III. For the next twenty years, he was in constant warfare with one group after another. Some of the activities that kept him busy included leading armies, crushing clans, devastating lands, demolishing castles, conquering cities, and (surprise!) signing peace treaties. If treaties didn't establish authority to his satisfaction, then he conducted sieges (some up to two years), cut water supplies to cities, imprisoned enemies, demanded ransom, torched ships, and murdered whomever.

Somewhere along the way, he promoted himself from emir to caliph of Cordoba on January 16, 929. With this action he became the political *and* religious leader of all Muslims in Islamic Spain. Abd-ar-Rahman III used his increased stature to build alliances and consolidate power. During his reign in the Middle Ages, Cordoba was established as the intellectual center of Western Europe.

As a caliph, he had a harem, of course. Some sources claimed he had two—a female harem of six thousand sex slaves and a smaller-sized male harem of teenage sex slaves. Toward the end of his life, he lamented, "I have now reigned above fifty years in victory or peace...power and pleasure...days of pure and genuine happiness...They amount to Fourteen" [*sic*].

Only fourteen days of happiness in fifty years? What did he do on those happy days? Wander a battlefield after a victory? Imitate his grandfather by executing a son who he thought had conspired against him? Rape a sex slave in one or both of his harems? (He reportedly dismembered a young boy who rejected his advances.) Abd-ar-Rahman III wrote that he "diligently numbered the days," but he does not indicate how he enjoyed those fourteen days. He left us in the dark in the Dark Ages.

[Exit Depravity.]

THE END: A Tragedy for All

EUROPEANS: MONARCHS, RELIGIOUS LEADERS, SLAVE TRADER

Henry the Navigator—White Ships, Black Slaves. A weary Europe stumbled into the fourteen hundreds reeling from a century or more of famine, climate change, war, trade jealousies, and Black Death:

- Food, once abundant, was scarce in the early thirteen hundreds due to prolonged periods of cold, rainy weather, which caused crops to fail for several decades.
- Portugal's *Reconquista* (the struggle to reclaim territory from the Moors) was achieved in 1249, although Christian-Muslim warfare continued in Islamic Spain until 1492, when the Moors lost Granada and retreated to North Africa.
- Venetian and Genoese merchants dominated trade routes from the Mediterranean Sea and into the Black Sea; their ships awaited slow-moving and bandit-prone caravans from the East, laden with spices, silks, and carpets.
- Some of these caravans from Central Asia carried the fleas with the disease that killed one-third or more of Europe's people, especially poor, from 1346 to 1353.
- This Black Death created a labor shortage for numerous businesses and affluent households and resulted in reviving the buying and selling of people.

Once again the demand for slaves exceeded the supply.

Since Portugal did not have a port on the Mediterranean, its merchants may have wondered if there were faster, safer, and more profitable routes than continuing to meet slow-moving caravans along the North African coast. Instead of sailing east between the Pillars of Hercules (Gibraltar) and into the Mediterranean to meet the caravans, why not head south along West Africa? Perhaps there were shortcuts in their search for gold, spices, and slaves. Some Portuguese sailors had ventured, apprehensively, as far south as Cape Bojador in West Africa, where, below this point, it was said that currents ran swiftly, winds blew forcefully, waves churned violently, sea monsters swam stealthily, and ships never returned.

Who was bold enough to attempt this kind of voyage?

Not Henry the Navigator. (He would enjoy *planning* future expeditions, not going on them!) However, before he could start planning them, there were immediate concerns in 1415 that Portugal needed to address in the Mediterranean: Barbary pirates were raiding coastal villages, capturing Europeans, and selling them into slavery in North Africa, Cairo, and other Middle East locations. The females became sex slaves in harems and homes, while the males were forced into hard labor or killed. Against this backdrop, Prince Henry (then twenty-one), his brothers, his father (Portugal's king), and Portuguese ships with soldiers seized Cueta, a Moorish port in northern Morocco used by the pirates. Henry stayed there for several months to learn about the African caravan trade of gold, silver, spices, textiles, and slaves. He wondered if he could circumvent the land routes by dispatching ships and acquiring these goods and slaves for Portugal before Muslims seize them? With improved navigational aids and newly designed ships, he/we could sail down the West Coast of Africa with confidence and courage to Cape Bojador and beyond.

In 1416 Henry established a base of operations and a school in Sagres, located on the southwest tip of Portugal on the Atlantic Ocean. The objective was to train people to explore the west coast of Africa and return with gold, goods, and slaves. Voyages would create income for Portugal and save the souls of slaves by persuading (coercing?) them to become Christians; a devout Roman Catholic, Prince Henry believed this to be true.

But first he had to design and build ships that could handle the currents, depths, and winds at Cape Bojador. The older *barcas* and Venetian *carracks*, commonly used for cargo, were designed to sail *with* the wind. For the return trip, a new, lighter, more maneuverable ship would have to sail *into* the wind. New ships would need shallower drafts, enabling them to come as close as possible to the coastline and explore up river. They would also need new sails; instead of fixed, square sails, the ships were fitted with more efficient *lateen*, or slanted and triangular, sails. The new ship design was called a caravel. Portuguese explorers loved it, but its cargo capacity was limited; the caravel carried fewer slaves than the older ships. Although it took nearly twenty years of planning, preparation, new ship building, and more than a dozen unsuccessful attempts, the Portuguese finally succeeded in sailing beyond Cape Bojador in 1434. Numerous voyages followed in the next half-dozen years.

By 1441, Prince Henry found himself and Portugal deeply involved in the Atlantic slave trade. However, by 1455 he concluded that the capturing of black Africans should cease. Maybe he finally realized that tearing families apart and enslaving their bodies was not an acceptable way of saving their souls. But, he had waited too long to object; the flow of gold and slaves had become too profitable to stop. Henry died in 1460, perhaps not fully realizing what he had set in motion. About twenty years after his death, Portugal started building Elmina Castle in Guinea on Africa's west coast. This "castle" became a trading outpost and slave factory; it was the first of many.

During the Atlantic slave trade, Portugal shipped 4,650,000 slaves on 30,000 voyages to Brazil, the Caribbean Islands, the British/American colonies, and the United States of America. That's 42.3 percent of the eleven million slaves sent to the New World and 55.3 percent of the total voyages. Somehow, it is hard to believe that the little Kingdom of Portugal shipped more slaves than any other European country to the New World. At its peak, however, the Portuguese Empire included about one-half of South America (Brazil), several colonies in Africa, and possessions in Asia and on the subcontinent of India. It was the world's first global empire, due largely to the persistent and skillful, although inadvertently infamous, efforts of Henry the Navigator.

The Roman Catholic Church, Papal Bulls, and Slavery. Portugal and Spain (unified in 1469 by the merger of Aragon and Castile), the Catholic Church, and Islam competed to extend their power and authority in Europe and throughout the world in the fourteen hundreds. After decades of costly warfare against several adversaries, the treasuries of Portugal and Spain were dwindling; they needed new income (increased taxes were not enough), not only for current operating expenses but also for funding the *Reconquista* that was slowly expelling the Moors from the Iberian Peninsula. At the same time, the Catholic Church wanted to spread Christianity to Africa, Asia, the Americas, and other unexplored lands as quickly as possible.

Several popes assumed political power by issuing papal bulls (a letter or charter issued by a pope of the Catholic Church on various topics, including slavery and overseas exploration). Some bulls authorized Portugal and Spain to conquer previously unknown territories and return with whatever goods they could gather. These might include gold, silver, textiles, spices, or slaves. The bulls provided a rationale to save the souls of innumerable slaves by converting them before the Muslims could. The power vacuum left behind by the fall of Rome in 476 was continuing to be vigorously contested, both militarily and theologically, one thousand years later.

Some of the papal bulls and popes were as follows:

June 18, 1452, ***Dum Diversas*, Nicholas V.** This bull authorized Alfonso V of Portugal to acquire and place any non-Christians—Saracens

(Muslims) and pagans—in perpetual slavery. This cleared the way for Portugal to plunder Africa.

January 5, 1455, *Romanus Pontifex*, Nicholas V. This broader bull gave the Catholic nations of Europe and, in particular, King Alfonso V of Portugal, dominion over discovered lands during the Age of Exploration, including Africa and the New World. In other words, seize the lands and enslave the natives; it's good for God, and us.

March 13, 1456, *Inter Caetera Quae*, Callixtus III. This reaffirmed the two previous bulls—*Dum Diversas* and *Romanus Pontifex*—but contradicted the position taken by Pope Eugene IV in the bull of January 13, 1435, *Sicut Dudum*, which prohibited enslaving natives in the Canary Islands who had converted or were converting to Christianity. This flip-flop, twenty-one years later, suggested a political tug-of-war going on between Portugal and the papacy concerning enslavement of natives, baptized or not.

June 21, 1481, *Aeterni Regis*, Sixtus IV. This bull combined the art of compromise, confirmation, and exploitation. It confirmed *Romanus Pontifex* and *Inter Caetera Quae* while agreeing with the Treaty of Alcáçovas (signed September 4, 1479). This treaty ended a civil war among Catholic monarchs in Iberia and granted Portugal domination of the Atlantic Ocean; it was one of the first international documents to empower European nations in their pursuit of *colonialism* during the Age of Exploration (or *Exploitation,* a more appropriate word?). Roaming free in their homeland, natives would soon be invaded by visitors bearing superior weapons who assumed they had the right to enslave and plunder for the glory of their king and queen.

In **1493** Pope Alexander IV issued three **Bulls of Donation** that, once again, confirmed and granted overseas lands to Portugal and Spain. These bulls were the basis for the Treaty of Tordesillas in 1494, which divided the largely unexplored New World between them by drawing a line of longitude, known as a meridian, in the Atlantic Ocean.

Lands east of the meridian were for Portugal, and those to the west for Spain. The kingdoms disagreed, of course, over the location of the meridian at 38° west longitude. Portugal argued that it had received too little land to the east, while Spain got too much land to the west. The meridian was then moved 8° westward to about 46° west longitude, a little bit west of the present city of Rio de Janeiro. Portugal would stretch this boundary by exploring the interior and naming the country Brazil. Meanwhile, Spain seized the rest of South America and spread northward into Central America and North America, including future American colonies.

The English, French, and Dutch ignored this unilateral papal pronouncement of a meridian as it applied to the northern coast of South America, Caribbean Islands, and North America. They concluded that papal bulls were politically meaningless and were eager to oppose them, even if it took a century or more.

Francisco Felix de Souza, Slave Trader, Early Eighteen Hundreds. Then, as today, time was money: the faster the passage, the quicker the payment. Fewer slaves died en route on shorter trips, and that meant greater profits. Sailing primarily in the South Atlantic, these ships delivered slaves in about four weeks from Ouidah in Dahomey to Bahia in Brazil. The ships returned with sugar, molasses, coffee, and gold in the same amount of time. Once in port, traders rounded up new slaves, hurried them on board, and repeated this nonstop voyage. These trips were thousands of miles shorter and several weeks fewer than routes of the triangular slave trade of the North Atlantic.

The man who initiated this profitable passage was Francisco de Souza. A Brazilian slave trader, de Souza worked for King Gezo of Dahomey, who was turning his empire into a major force in the West African slave trade. (Gezo was mentioned earlier in this chapter.) De Souza had helped Gezo overthrow his brother, Abandonzan, in 1818 to become king. Gezo rewarded de Souza by appointing him viceroy in charge of slave trade for the Kingdom of Dahomey. As a result, de Souza was considered by many to be the most successful dealer of slaves on the Bight of Benin.

De Souza was born in 1769 in Brazil, a Portuguese colony that became independent in 1825. He arrived in Ouidah (a city in present-day Benin) in 1792, when he was twenty-three. After several years in Ouidah, de Souza returned to Brazil only to reappear in Ouidah around 1800. He started as a slave trader, but that lasted for just a few years. Then he got a job at the Portuguese fort (slave factory) in 1803 where his brother, Jacinto, was appointed governor in 1804. During the next three years, de Souza worked his way up from scribe to bookkeeper to storekeeper. When his brother and then his brother's successor died, de Souza ended up as governor. But that job may not have been exciting enough, because he left after a while to become a slave trader again.

By the time de Souza resumed slave trading, it had become an illegal activity. Great Britain, the next largest slave-trading nation after Portugal, unilaterally abolished the trans-Atlantic slave trade in 1807 in the North Atlantic, and, by 1820, in the South Atlantic. The British navy, which then ruled the seas, enforced the law by imposing fines, confiscating ships, and freeing slaves. Despite this threat to their business, de Souza and several other traders continued to buy, sell, and ship slaves for the next twenty years from Africa to Brazil and even to Cuba. To sustain this activity, de Souza bought confiscated ships and reconditioned condemned ones. He and other traders apparently concluded that the risk was worth the reward.

Profitable voyages allowed de Souza to live lavishly, entertain extravagantly, and become an influential businessman. Although married, he maintained a harem of a thousand sex slaves—white, brown, black—who provided him with some eighty children. The result of rape? What else would it be?

Since 1818 de Souza's arrangement with King Gezo paid him handsomely for many years. Then the good times began to ebb. By the early 1840s, de Souza owed substantial sums of money to merchants in Brazil and Cuba. The British navy captured more than twenty of his slave ships, freed slaves, and levied fines, depriving him of thousands of dollars of profit. To make matters worse, he owed King Gezo a lot of money and was eventually replaced as viceroy. His life had lost its luster.

De Souza died on May 8, 1849, at age eighty. Since he was a Catholic who dabbled in the Vodun cult (voodoo), King Gezo thought about giving him an official Dahomey funeral including the offering of a human sacrifice. His family objected. This kind of funeral would have symbolized de Souza's career—built on the suffering of slaves whose families and futures were sacrificed on an altar of greed.

AMERICANS: FOUNDING LEADERS, SLAVE STATES, REBELLIOUS SLAVES

The Land of the Free and the Home of the Slave. Five of eight men commonly considered as our "founding leaders" owned slaves; two did not; and one was somewhere in between. These eight men were discussed in two books about "founding fathers" and "founding brothers" written, respectively, by historians Richard B. Morris and Joseph J. Ellis. (They each chose the same six men, while suggesting a different seventh one as a founding father or brother, for a total of eight.) Four of the slave owners are names familiar to most of us: George Washington, Thomas Jefferson, James Madison, and Benjamin Franklin; the fifth slave owner was John Jay, our first chief justice of the Supreme Court (Morris's seventh *founding father*). The two who did not own slaves were Aaron Burr (Ellis's seventh *founding brother*) and John Adams. The eighth founding father/brother mutually agreed upon by Morris and Ellis was Alexander Hamilton, who married into a prominent slaveholding family, but did not own slaves himself. Since he believed in protecting property rights, which included the owning of slaves, he straddled this dilemma.

As you read the brief biographies below, remember that our new nation, emerging from the British/American colonies, was not only a *slave-owning society* but also a *slave society* in Upper and Deep South states and territories starting in 1619.

The American Experience began in 1607 when Captain John Smith and 104 white settlers founded a British/American colony in Jamestown, Virginia. In 1619 twenty black slaves joined them, initiating a slave-owning society for the next 246 years until the Civil War ended and ratification of the 13th Amendment to the Constitution abolished slavery on December 6, 1865. The 246 years of slavery from 1619 to 1865 are *60 percent* of our entire 409-year history (1607 to 2016) as a colony/country. Therefore, our society has been the Land of the Free for *only 40 percent* of our history. Hard to believe, but true; do the math. Fortunately, time is on our side to set things right. As each year passes, we increase the number of years that we have been the Land of the Free and the Home of the Brave (not the slave). We're headed in the right direction, although it may take a while to get there.

Why did people flee tyranny in Europe and impose it here for generations? Similar to human trafficking in ancient Athens and imperial Rome, they brought to America a profit-driven business model based on slavery, rape, and greed. Yet, some of these slave owners were among our greatest patriots who helped gain our nation's freedom from Great Britain. Here are three:

George Washington. Our first president was born in 1732 on a Virginia tobacco plantation on the Northern Neck (peninsula) that jutted into the Chesapeake Bay. The area attracted wealthy planters, who formed an elite society that became known as the "Athens of the New World." Like Athenian aristocrats, they valued education, civic responsibilities, and freedom for themselves, while relying on slave labor for income. Many leaders of our revolution grew up here, surrounded with black slaves from Africa.

At age eleven, George inherited ten slaves when his father died. By age twenty-two he had assumed control of Mount Vernon and owned eighteen slaves. When George married Martha, a wealthy widow, on January 6, 1759, he acquired two hundred more slaves. By investing his wife's wealth in land, Washington tripled the size of Mount Vernon's acreage and bought additional slaves to farm it; three hundred slaves were at Mount Vernon when he died, December 14, 1799. Among the southern slaveholding founding leaders, Washington was the only one to free all his slaves in his will. However, they were not to be freed upon his death, but upon his wife's. Martha didn't wait that long. She freed them twelve months after he died.

Benjamin Franklin. Franklin owned slaves, as few as two, as many as five. They were servants in his Philadelphia home and newspaper shop. Ben also "supported" slavery by selling ads in his newspaper regarding the sale of slaves and the search for fugitives. While the vast majority of slaves labored on southern plantations, black slaves and indentured white servants worked in Boston, Newport, New York, Philadelphia, and other northern cities as laborers, coachmen, craftsmen, and household domestics. Slavery was widespread throughout the colonies.

In retrospect, it seems surprising that Franklin held a slavery mindset. He was a self-made American: a person of humble beginnings who became highly educated; a possessor of a fertile, curious, ingenious mind; a printer, inventor, author, scientist, diplomat, and innovator of civic improvements—a public hospital, a volunteer fire department, a college known today as the University of Pennsylvania. Yet, he had difficulty recognizing the contradiction of enslaving people for work in the colonies while he and others demanded freedom for our nation from Great Britain. Gradually he realized this inconsistency, and by 1770 had freed his slaves. Then Franklin became an antislavery activist at home and internationally.

Thomas Jefferson. When it came to the subject of slavery, Jefferson seemed more literary than literal: "We hold these Truths to be self-evident, that all Men are created equal..." Blacks weren't treated equally then or today, despite his inspiring rhetoric in our Declaration of Independence.

Jefferson was born into the planter class of a slaveholding society in 1743. When he was eleven, his father died, leaving an estate of five thousand acres, cattle, buildings, and fifty-two slaves. Thomas inherited these at age twenty-one. In 1772, when he was twenty-eight, he married a widow, Martha Wayles. Her father died the next year, and the couple inherited two plantations and 135 slaves, including an infant named Sally Hemings. (See next *When Thomas Met Sally*.)

Although Jefferson owned hundreds of slaves during his lifetime, he tried to ban slavery in the new territories of the North and South. But the "no slavery" clause in the federal legislation he introduced in the US Congress, the Ordinance of 1784, failed by *one* vote. Following this defeat, his official duties increased, and he had less time for antislavery efforts. When he died on July 4, 1826, he freed only a handful of slaves in his will. A year later the remaining 130 slaves at Monticello were sold to pay the debts of Jefferson's estate.

When Thomas Met Sally—Consent or Rape? Thomas Jefferson could have been an aristocratic slave owner in ancient Athens, as well as one in the American colony of Virginia. His manner, bearing, knowledge of literature and the arts, and passion for the freedom of our emerging nation seemed consistent with the interests of elite Athenians. Even his "blind spot" on slavery was similar to theirs. There was a difference, however. Jefferson was truly troubled by the widespread practice of slavery (hence, the Ordinance of 1784), whereas most Athenian aristocrats could not have cared less. They accepted slavery as the normal plight of some, as long as *they* weren't the slaves.

Numerous American slave owners identified with ancient Athenians in another way—by adopting the Greek slave-owner custom of *rape*. Many married Virginia planters numbered slave children among their white offspring; southern mores merely asked them to be discreet. While married, Jefferson chose not to have sex with his slaves. His wife, Martha, died after childbirth in 1782, and he never remarried. Later in life, he fathered slave children as a widower with Sally Hemings.

But let's begin a few generations earlier with Sally's grandmother, Susanna, a black African, and her grandfather, an English sea captain named John Hemings. They had a daughter, Betty, who was born 50 percent black and 50 percent white (aka mulatto). Susanna and Betty were both owned by a man named Francis Eppes IV, who refused to sell them to Hemings. When Eppes died, his daughter, Martha, inherited them, and they became her personal servants. When Martha Eppes married John Wayles, an Englishman, the two servants went along with her into the Wayles household. The first child of John and Martha Eppes Wayles was also named Martha, and she eventually married Thomas Jefferson.

When Martha Eppes Wayles died, her husband and now widower, John Wayles, inherited Susanna and Betty Hemings. He remarried twice more, and both wives died. Instead of marrying a fourth time, he turned to Betty Hemings, his mulatto slave, for sex and, quite possibly, solace. They had six children in twelve years; the youngest was Sally. Since his slave children were now three-quarters white, their skin was rather fair. John Wayles died in 1773 (the same year Sally was born). His daughter, Martha, and son-in-law, Thomas Jefferson, inherited eleven thousand acres and 135 slaves, including the Hemings family. Sally, an infant, was twenty-nine years younger than Thomas Jefferson.

In 1784, two years after his wife died, Jefferson was appointed the American envoy to France. His oldest daughter, named Martha (aka Patsy), accompanied him to Paris. He left two younger daughters, Lucy and Maria (aka Polly), with friends in the United States. Lucy died of whooping cough in 1787. Distraught over Lucy's death, Jefferson sent for his last daughter in America, nine-year-old Maria. He wanted her to live with him in France. Maria's servant and traveling companion was a teenage slave named Sally Hemings.

After the French Revolution in 1789, slavery was abolished in France, and Sally could have stayed there and petitioned for her freedom. However, she was sixteen and pregnant by Jefferson. Who would she turn to? Where would she live? How would she support herself? Faced with unanswerable questions, she returned with Jefferson from Paris to the United States as a slave. The baby died soon after their return. Sally would have six children with Jefferson, with two of them dying. Since her surviving children were seven-eighths white, they moved easily throughout the white community as they reached adulthood.

Did Sally's sexual relationship with Thomas Jefferson begin with consent or rape? She was sixteen years old; he was forty-five and a very important person in the American government. Did she go along to get along? Did she gain a more protected life by being a sex slave to her owner? Remember the definition of a slave at the beginning of this book: *a human being who is owned as property by another and is absolutely subject to his will.* Could there have been genuine mutual affection, if not love, between the two of them? Maybe, but we don't know, at least not yet. What we do know is that she was a slave, and he was her owner—and slaves were compelled to do what their owners demanded (or requested?)—whether or not they lived in ancient Athens, imperial Rome, or a mansion in Virginia known as Monticello.

Fourteen Slave Societies in the American South. By 1860, fourteen of fifteen southern states were "slave societies." The slave population in fourteen southern states was more than 20 percent per state (United States 1860 census, modified below). These slaves produced a significant amount of agricultural products—indigo, tobacco, sugarcane, cotton, wheat, rice, corn, and other vegetables. Applying Keith Hopkins's definition of *population* (at least 20 percent slave) and *production* (substantial), each state was a *slave society*. They shared this dubious designation with ancient Athens, imperial Rome, Brazil, Cuba, and Saint-Domingue (Haiti).

Deep South States (8)	Percent of Slaves in State Population (1860)
South Carolina	57.2
Mississippi	55.2
Louisiana	46.8
Alabama	45.1
Florida	43.9
Georgia	43.7
Texas	30.2
Arkansas	25.5

Upper South States (7) plus Washington, DC	
North Carolina	33.4
Virginia	30.7
Tennessee	24.8
Kentucky	19.5 (some sources claim 25%)

Maryland	12.7 (in 1755, 40% slaves)
Missouri	9.7 (in 1821, a slave state)
Wash., DC (not a state)	4.2 (in 1862, slaves freed)
Delaware (not a slave society)	1.6 (free black, 17.7%)

(*Note: although the 1860 census shows the population of Kentucky and Maryland as having fewer than 20 percent slaves, they were slave societies; additional research verifies this. Missouri, aka Little Dixie, was admitted to the Union as a slave state; its slave population in twenty-three counties ranged from 20 to 50 percent.*)

Relying on slave labor, plantations multiplied and enlarged to provide owners, slave traders, and investors with increased revenue and profit. In the late 1700s, these groups realized continual wealth through Article 1, Section 9, of the US Constitution (ratified 1788), which protected the import slave trade until January 1, 1808. This date roughly coincided with Great Britain's decision to end the trans-Atlantic slave trade in 1807. However, the practice of slavery *within* America continued; more than one million slaves walked in chains from the Upper South to the Deep South (Virginia to Mississippi) until the Civil War ended in 1865.

Owners of large plantations used cruelty and intimidation to control dozens, if not hundreds, of slaves. Why? Whites lived in constant fear of rebellion. To maintain control, the white elite used chains, dogs, guns, whips, lynching, militia, local law enforcement, and federal troops. When rebellions occurred, they were usually crushed within a few days, and many slaves were arrested or executed for planning and participating in them.

Three Major Slave Uprisings in the 19th Century. America, as Rome, had its share of slave rebellions. However, these involved generally hundreds of slaves, not thousands, as with Rome. Also, Rome's slave rebellions lasted years, not days.

1811, Louisiana, on Mississippi River. On January 8, a slave revolt began on a sugarcane plantation along the east bank of the Mississippi River north of New Orleans. The slaves injured the owner and reportedly killed his son. With farm implements as weapons and some firearms, the band of slaves marched to the next plantation, recruiting members. Then they continued to another plantation, gathering more slaves. A planter was killed with an axe; a home was torched. They moved on to more plantations. The rebels now numbered about two hundred. Meanwhile slaveholders, local militia, and government troops formed a group that attacked and suppressed the rebellion within three days. More than one hundred slaves died in battle; trials convicted dozens more; others were released to their masters; many were hanged. Some slaves were decapitated and their heads impaled on pikes in front of plantations and on the banks of the Mississippi River for mile after mile to New Orleans.

Why did a rebellion occur? Various reasons:

1. By 1799 the French Revolution had abolished slavery in its colonies, spreading liberalism and democracy worldwide.
2. By 1804 a revolt in Saint-Domingue (Haiti) had won independence from France, encouraging slaves in America to consider rebelling.
3. In 1808 the United States ended its participation in the trans-Atlantic slave trade, offering hope to antislavery efforts in America.
4. In September 1810, an unsuccessful uprising in Mexico of poor farmers armed only with sticks, stones, and machetes continued to fan the flames of freedom.

5. In January 1811, for those families in perpetual slavery along the Mississippi River in Louisiana, when was enough, enough?

1822, South Carolina, Denmark Vesey. A former slave, Denmark Vesey (1767–July 2, 1822) could read, write, and speak three languages—English, French, and Spanish. He also earned a good living as a free black carpenter. So why would Vesey jeopardize his freedom and his life by planning a slave revolt? Since he had bought his own freedom at age thirty-two, he had anticipated buying freedom for his wife and children. But her slave owner refused to sell them to him, angering Vesey.

Then in 1818, instead of continuing to worship with a black minority in a white church in Charleston, he helped start a black church. It soon numbered nearly two thousand members, including slaves. Such a large group bothered city officials. They also felt the church violated the local slave code by teaching slaves to read and by meeting after sunset. So, officials closed the church a few times, the last one in 1821. Vesey's latent anger boiled over. In *Rebels against Slavery*, 1996, Patricia C. and Frederick L. McKissack quote Vesey as saying, after the church closed, "We were deprived of our rights and privileges by the white people… Our church was shut up so that we could not use it…It was high time for us to seek our rights…and we were fully able to conquer the whites if we were only unanimous and courageous as the Santo Domingo [Haitian] people were."

Key actions of the rebellion were to start fires in the city as distractions; seize firearms and ammunition; kill slave owners and free their slaves; and capture ships in the harbor and sail to freedom, maybe Haiti. But plans went awry. Some people snitched, and the conspiracy was quashed before it started. About 130 slaves were arrested. Thirty-five were hanged, including Vesey. His black church was demolished. Another one wasn't built in Charleston until after the Civil War.

1831, Virginia, Nat Turner. Mystery surrounds the birth and life of Nat Turner (October 2, 1800–November 11, 1831). Historians debate whether his mother, a black African slave in her late teens, arrived in America on a slave ship in the 1790s or was brought here with her owner from Saint-Domingue (Haiti) while fleeing that island's revolution of 1791–1804. Regardless of how she got here, she ended up on a Virginia plantation owned by Benjamin Turner. He named her Nancy Turner.

Within a few years she became pregnant, either by a slave who later escaped or by Ben Turner (rape?); historians differ. Ben called the baby Nathaniel. Some sources said Nat was dark skinned, while others claimed light skinned. A gifted child, he learned to read at an early age. Ben, his owner (and father?), a Methodist, encouraged him to read the Bible. Nat embraced Christianity and decided to be a preacher and a prophet who advocated freedom for all, especially slaves.

From his early teens until his mid twenties, he had visions of white and black "spirits" battling each other, while voices called upon him to lead. In the 1820s, he married. Early in the marriage, he and his wife were sold along with farm animals and implements to *different* owners to settle an estate. This cruel separation added to Nat's embittered feelings toward white slaveholders. By 1828, when his visions intensified, Nat convinced himself that he had been selected by God to lead a major rebellion. Signs from the skies would tell him when the time had come. Until that day arrived, voices told him to keep preaching and planning an uprising, but to confide it only to a few people. Within three years the heavens spoke.

A solar eclipse of one minute and fifty-seven seconds occurred on February 11, 1831. The moon covered 98 percent of the sun, leaving a fiery, circular ring around a black moon. Nat saw this as a black hand obscuring the sun and indicating that the time to act was near. He had planned a rebellion for Independence Day, July 4, but postponed it due to illness and a need for more discussion with four trusted slaves. Then, on August 13, another heavenly sign appeared—a bluish-green Sun. (A solar eclipse? Volcanic ash from a Mount Saint Helens eruption?)

On August 21, 1831, Nat Turner began his uprising. It was bloody and brutal for whites (sixty men, women, and children killed) and blacks (fifty-six executed by the state and up to two hundred—many were innocent bystanders—killed by white militias and mobs). The rebellion was over in a few days. Nat was on the run for two months before being captured, convicted, and hanged.

The aftermath of Nat Turner's Rebellion was far-reaching: Cries increased to resettle blacks to Africa. Antislavery movements slowed. Rights were stripped from free blacks. New state laws prohibited education of slaves. Fears of rebellions accelerated. Slavery became more repressive than ever. Would it ever end? Yes. Thirty-four years and 625,000 deaths later, our Civil War ended slavery...with liberty and justice for all. Right?

CONCLUSION

Power Corrupts

IN AN APRIL 5, 1887 letter, Lord Acton, an English writer, politician, and historian wrote, "Power tends to corrupt, and absolute power corrupts absolutely. Great men are almost always bad men, even when they exercise influence and not authority."

Here are some thoughts about the exercise of power by men in this chapter:

We have had a ringside seat on the use or abuse of royal, political, financial, theological, and sexual power. We have seen how slavery, rape, and greed were exported around the world from Africa, expanding the sordid evolution of human trafficking.

Is Lord Acton correct? Does power corrupt? What do you think?

In Part Three: Sex Slaves of Today's World, we'll see how pimps and human traffickers have exercised *absolute power that corrupts absolutely.*

PART THREE
Sex Slaves of Today's World

PREFACE

Is She Your Missing Daughter?

(A fictitious composite based on real life)

"Get up," he said. "You have a visitor."

She stirred, tried to rise, but she was tired. She was always tired, and naked. Her last "visitor" had left twenty minutes ago, leaving her tired and naked. For months she has been tired and naked—ever since she was abducted on her way home from school in a little town in Texas. Two men had stopped their car. There was no one in sight on this late spring day. They grabbed her. She fought. They were too strong. She thought she would be raped. They didn't do that until later: until they were miles away; until news reports ended; until no remains were found; until police stopped searching for her. Until her grief-stricken parents had wondered over and over and over again what did we do wrong? Did she run away? Is she dead?

She was alive in a living hell, where she was raped several times a day. By white men, black men, brown men. By young men, middle-aged men, and older men. By men with diamond rings on their pinkies and others with wedding bands. Sometimes, by two men at once, their tailored clothes hanging on a rack on the wall behind them. Some were wealthy, educated. You could sense it in their demeanor. Others were paunchy, thin, or muscular. Some had hairy bodies; others had smooth skin. Some looked like the boy next door, others too frightful to imagine. It only mattered that they had the money to buy her time. She was not a prostitute. She was a sex slave. Sold to her owner by the men who had kidnapped her. She was a replaceable part in a profitable business model known today as *human trafficking*, involving more than 140 countries around the world.

"Get up," he said again, "your visitor is waiting. Time is money. I have a business to run."

CHAPTER 4

International Sex Trade

And lead us not into temptation,
but deliver us from evil: For thine
is the kingdom, and the power, and
the glory, for ever. Amen.
—MATTHEW 6:13

HUMAN TRAFFICKING IN THE 21ST CENTURY

GLOBAL HUMAN TRAFFICKING OF WOMEN, children, and men results in forced labor (slavery) and coerced sex (rape). Either servitude produces sizable profits (greed) for slave owners and slave traders. Human-trafficking victims have been befriended falsely, kidnapped, sold, drugged, beaten, tied up, raped, and oftentimes killed. Their tragic plight is similar to that of the slaves of thousands of years ago in Athens and Rome, and hundreds of years ago in Africa, Middle Eastern countries, Europe, Brazil, and America.

Human trafficking—with its evil business practices—has persisted for centuries, while penalties have lagged far behind. Laws are catching up with the lawless, although it has taken more than a hundred years for this to happen in America and elsewhere:

- In 1902, delegates from sixteen European nations met in Paris and passed the International Agreement for the Suppression of the White Slave Traffic.
- In 1910, prodded by suffrage activists and groups, the US Congress passed the White-Slave Traffic Act, commonly known as the Mann Act. Named after its sponsor, James R. Mann of Illinois, it was one of several pieces of moral reform law in the early twentieth century.
- In 1921, the League of Nations held a convention that redefined the crime of white slavery, expanding it to include the trafficking of women and children of various ethnicities and races.

Despite these acts and laws, human trafficking continued to expand in the twentieth century. Then, in 1949, the United Nations sponsored a convention to address the abuse of women and children. Forty-nine countries ratified a report that drew a direct link between sex trafficking and prostitution. Without an effective monitoring mechanism, however, a UN commitment for justice was powerless to contain the spread of human trafficking during the next fifty years. In fact, some UN members ignored the convention's provisions and weakened their own laws.

Private organizations stepped forward to help. From 1950 until 2000, numerous local and global antislavery groups (some estimates claim nearly eight hundred groups) were formed to create awareness of sex trafficking. During these years, local, regional, national, and international law enforcement agencies identified and arrested many pimps and human-trafficking traders. The international sex trade continued to grow, however, because the reward was greater than the risk—penalties were not severe enough.

As we entered the twenty-first century, several conferences urged action:

- In 2000, the UN Convention against Transnational Organized Crime agreed on a comprehensive international definition of trafficking.
- In 2004, the Association of Southeast Asian Nations (ASEAN) adopted a Declaration against Trafficking in Persons Particularly Women and Children.
- In 2005, the Council of Europe in Warsaw issued a Declaration and Action Plan Against Trafficking in Human Beings.
- In 2006, the African Union created a plan to Combat Trafficking in Human Beings.
- In 2007, the United Nations launched the Global Initiative to Fight Human Trafficking.
- In 2008, the United Nations invited a universal exchange of views on June 3 at a New York City seminar on human trafficking. One delegate asked a troubling question: "With all these laws and international agreements in place, why is the problem getting worse?"

Delegates responded: Criminal networks now operate on a global scale. Human trafficking affects all societies and all regions of the world, developed and developing. Easy means of global communication and transport help criminals. There is increased demand for cheap labor and services, particularly from the sex industry. Social and economic conditions make people vulnerable to traffickers/pimps.

Delegates recommended: We must raise global awareness of trafficking. We need closer cross-border cooperation to catch and prosecute traffickers. We need to partner with private sectors to prevent forced labor and trafficking. We must put in place a regular review mechanism to hold member states and the UN system to account. We need to lift people out of poverty.

Words, words, words.

Citizens and Cops Turn Words into Action

On November 6, 2012, 81 percent of the voters of California seized the initiative and passed Proposition 35, Ban on Human Trafficking and Sex Slavery. Prop 35 imposed some of the strictest criminal penalties on traffickers and pimps to date. Two key components of the law were the following: (1) increased prison sentences from fifteen years to life and (2) fines up to $1.5 million. Although severe, these penalties have not adequately decreased the crime of human trafficking that steals many years from a victim's life while subjecting sex slaves to unimaginable abuse and daily rape.

Here's a Draconian remedy: perhaps the perpetrators should be chemically castrated, fined, and imprisoned. Is this too severe? What do you think? Read deeply about human trafficking; learn of the psychological and physical abuse of children, women, and men; ask yourself, should courts and law enforcement deal more harshly with these predators?

In America, 2014 was a good year for arresting pimps and freeing children and women. Thanks to the FBI and local police officers in New York-New Jersey, 45 pimps were arrested and 16 kids rescued; in Washington, DC, 281 pimps were arrested and 168 children rescued; in several southern California cities, including Los Angeles, more than 100 pimps were arrested and dozens of kids saved.

In other parts of our country, a pimp, age thirty-two, was sentenced to life imprisonment in Georgia on six counts of trafficking persons for sexual servitude. In Virginia, a pimp, thirty-four, received forty years in prison for sex trafficking a child. In New York City, two out of three pimps were sentenced to eighteen years each, while the third received ten years. And yet pimps, assuming they won't be caught, continue to enslave children, women, and men. If neither lengthy prison terms nor sizable fines deter them, then the primary penalty could be more severe. And everlasting.

Consider this timely news item: a Utah state lawmaker sought a permanent penalty—death—for sex traffickers of children. Representative Paul Ray suggested the idea in 2014. His proposed legislation was approved February 2, 2016 by a panel of Utah lawmakers, 6-3, for discussion by the Utah House and Senate. Although Ray recently revised his proposal to conform to Utah's other capital punishment laws, death penalty opponents felt the proposal was unjust. Also, Utah has a law that permits child abusers to face the death penalty, if they cause a child's death unintentionally but recklessly. In retrospect, Ray's well-intentioned bill may not be necessary. Originally he wanted to impose the death penalty even if sexually abused children did not die; this would have sent a strong message to pimps and human traffickers.

From Street Pimps to Elite Pimps

As I read more and more about pimps, I was dismayed to learn American decency has been debased by the celebration of pimps in several movies. It's hard to believe that some reviewers have labeled these as "memorable" pimp movies, considering that they extol street pimps who abuse women and children psychologically and physically while selling their bodies as sex slaves. Of course, the opportunity to glorify street pimps would not exist without elite pimps who create pornographic movies that peddle this debasement as art imitating life.

Whether a pimp is involved in the movie or not, some mainstream writers and producers seem unconcerned about showing a woman getting smacked across the face, put in her place (whatever that means), or worse. When a story line seems dull, just include more acts of violence against females. Tie them up. Beat them black and blue. Too many audiences, desensitized to abuse, accept it as "entertainment."

It's "entertainment" that spills out onto the streets, where it gets replayed nightly in towns and cities all across America. And, it's not art imitating life; it's artfulness for the sake of profit. It's the entertainment industry picking our pockets and inducing our minds to become accustomed to violence against women. Many people, however, refuse to accept this packaged perversion as art in movies and on television. Listen to their voices.

But before you hear them, permit me to mention another form of "entertainment" in America. Rap. In particular, a song titled "P.I.M.P." This rap, described as a significant success by some, was recorded by a hip-hop artist who characterizes himself as a "motherf**king P.I.M.P." The lyrics underscore the psychological strategy of pimps with the assertion "I'm your friend, your father, and confidant, bitch." Once the girl becomes his sex slave, he raps, "This ho you can have her, when I'm done I ain't gon' keep her."

This kind of rap is rot that eats away, every day, causing decay of decency today, and encourages violence against women. Now, hear their voices protesting violence as art.

Violence against Women in Film and on TV

On March 20, 2014, Jessica West, practicum student at Battered Women's Support Services in Vancouver, BC, Canada, posted an e-mail article titled "Violence against Women, Onscreen and Real Life." Here are excerpts:

> Scenes of violence against women (VAW) are ubiquitous in Hollywood: an episode of *Criminal Minds* features a psychopath who takes pleasure in torturing young teenage girls, an episode of *CSI* sees the detectives discovering the mangled body of a woman in a dumpster…The low-class ladies' maid on *Downton Abbey* is raped to spice up her character's plot line.

We consume these images as entertainment without questioning how they impact us or other people who watch them... The Parents Television Council found that between 2004 and 2009 scenes of violence against women on TV increased by 120%...

On March 7, the Vancouver International Women in Film Festival convened a panel to discuss the depiction of violence against women in film and television. Angela Marie MacDougall, Executive Director of Battered Women's Support Services, moderated the panel; panelists were Jarrah Hodge, creator of the Gender Focus blog, Arlana Green from WAVAW, Hilla Kerner from Vancouver Rape Relief and Women's Shelter, and Natalie Hill from Women Action and the Media Vancouver.

The first concern of the panel was how onscreen violence dehumanizes women. Arlana critiqued the way in which depictions of violence against women on screen dehumanize women by showing women's bodies as objects which men are entitled to. This dehumanization of women is the first step in justifying violence against them. She argued that TV and films therefore perpetuate violence against girls and women because the images we see on screen inform our behavior in real life.

Central to any criticism of depictions of violence against women in film and television is the fact that Hollywood is dominated by men, and the stories of rape, violence, and murder of women are being written, directed, and produced by men, for a male audience, in order to profit male executives in the film and television industry...That these depictions cater to men's sexual fantasies is disgusting and horrifying. And that the brutalization of women's bodies is being commodified to make money for men with privilege is something that we all should be concerned about.

Another concern, *not part of this panel discussion*, involves pimp-controlled, underage sex slaves, forced into prostitution, who face off-screen, real-life violence every day. For years they have been viewed as criminals instead of victims. Today, many state lawmakers have realized these minors should be treated with dignity and respect and protected by legislation known as safe harbor laws.

State Safe Harbor Laws and "John" Schools

Safe harbor laws have been enacted by several states to save sexually exploited children under age eighteen from being charged with prostitution. The first state to pass a safe harbor law was New York in 2008. Connecticut, Washington State, Texas, and Illinois followed in 2010. Tennessee and Minnesota voted for it in 2011. More states are moving to adopt safe harbor laws, usually introduced for legislative discussion in two versions—full or partial.

The "full" version provides underage sex slaves with immunity from arrest (pimps coerced them into prostitution) and offers support services to help them heal physically and psychologically (pimps, as well as johns, have beaten them up and raped them). In 2015, the Polaris Project reported that fifteen states have enacted "full" safe harbor laws, and seven states have voted for "partial" laws. Polaris, a nonprofit, nongovernmental organization in Washington, DC, seeks to end modern-day slavery.

The "partial" law provides either immunity or help in healing, but not both. Since state support services would need additional funds, some legislators might feel there is not enough money in annual budgets to help damaged kids heal. According to some estimates, there are about 100,000 children in the American commercial sex trade—girls and boys abused by kidnappers, pimps, and johns. It's a business that turns children into sex objects for sale, ages them prematurely, and replaces them when they become worn out. Putting a stop to this shamefulness requires help from legislators in all states; may they find funds to make kids healthy again.

In addition, state safe harbor laws should provide aggressive prosecution of pimps and johns. As reported earlier (you might go back and review "Citizens and Cops"), pimps are being put away for longer prison terms than ever.

Now, let's zero in on "johns," a common term for males who buy sex. They could be single, engaged, or married. If they bought sex from a coerced teen, their arrest should be for *rape*, and that could put them in jail for decades.

Schools for Johns. For years, johns had it easy. If caught with a prostitute, she would go to jail, and he would go home with maybe a wink and a slap on the wrist. Then most of the judges and the police were male, and, after all, boys will be boys. If the john was married, his wife probably wouldn't have known that he had sought sex on the streets. If a father, his children wouldn't have known either.

Today, however, the person he is having sex with could be a pimp-controlled, teenage sex slave, perhaps the age of a young daughter or son. Now, when arrested, instead of being charged with paying a prostitute for services, the john could be punished under sex-trafficking charges and face years in jail. His car might be impounded. He might be compelled to attend john school, an alternative to criminal prosecution or a condition of probation. The school could be as short as only one day. A fee would be charged to help cover costs. Discussion topics at the john school include risks of sexually transmitted diseases, possible violence toward johns or others, and effects on your family (especially, if you are married) and your community.

John schools—together with publicity, increased fines, and more severe sentences (sometimes repeat johns receive harsher sentences)—are designed to reduce the return of johns to the streets, seeking sex. In other words, go after the buyer, as well as the human traffickers and pimps.

Once demand decreases, so may the supply.

Archaic Court Rules vs. Human Trafficking Victims

Despite many convictions achieved by law enforcement agencies, prosecutors are often hampered by restrictive court procedures that favor traffickers and pimps who are mostly male. For example, in April 2015 in Texas, a sex trafficker of a minor (age fifteen) was charged on three different counts of sexual assault. Early in their relationship, he gave her meth and cocaine. After she was hooked, her need for more drugs was met only when she performed sex acts with several men. Although DNA verified these acts, the trafficker was convicted on a lesser charge. Why? Here are a few reasons, as well as some suggested reforms:

1. Victims Are Legally "Victimized." Defense lawyers are permitted to verbally assault a human trafficking victim with a barrage of questions for hours. These lawyers are interested in two things: discrediting the victim (even if she might be the age of one of their teenage daughters) and pocketing big fat fees provided by the trafficker. The money for the fees may have been collected from customers who purchased coerced sex from the fifteen-year-old girl, as well as other sex slaves. Defense lawyers may be reaping rape revenue (dirty money) resulting from the business of human trafficking.

Suggested Reform: In human trafficking cases, the sex victim should be able to present a complete story for the jury and judge to evaluate, not just answer questions; new court procedures should accommodate this. Also, it should be unethical and illegal for defense fees to be paid from trafficker income. If the wives and children of trafficker defense lawyers knew about this dirty money, I wonder what they would say?

2. *Traffickers Are Legally "Protected."* Since the trafficker is not required to testify during his trial, the "playing field" is not level. Also, since all aspects of the victim's life are revealed to the jury and judge, the trafficker's life should be, too. This should also include the lives of his lawyers.

Suggested Reform: The jury and judge should receive complete biographical and financial information on the trafficker and his lawyers. What is their net worth? How many homes do each own and where are they located? How many cars do each own and what are they? Who else have the trafficker's lawyers represented? What were the judgments? Traffickers and lawyers should be subjected to full disclosure. This information should also be given to all media in a handout.

Mandatory Disclosure: The jury and judge should be told how human traffickers and pimps enrich themselves (greed) by enslaving children, women, and men and selling their bodies for sexual purposes (rape) as well as for forced labor (slavery).

3. *Many Jurors Lack Knowledge of Human Trafficking.* Broken homes and broken dreams of childhood feed the business of human trafficking. Unloved, unhappy kids on the loose from impersonal or poverty-stricken homes are prey for hyenas of our society. They know where to find, entrap with drugs, and emotionally/physically/sexually abuse kids. For 100,000 children annually, this is an American Nightmare.

Will they ever experience the American Dream?

Unfortunately, the average American is unaware of the business of human trafficking. It is widespread but hidden; distant but nearby. All around us, children are ensnared by HT and oftentimes die. Magazines, newspapers, and TV report this as part of a weekly, daily, nightly blur of news; just one more story we, the people, seem unable to do anything about. After all, pimps and traffickers are not in our neighborhoods. Right?

How wrong we are.

Suggested Reform: As human trafficking increases, we must turn our legal system on its head when considering these cases. Instead of presuming innocence, let's presume guilt when prima facie evidence is gathered, as in this case. People implicated of human trafficking should be put in the position of proving their innocence, not the other way around. For too long our system has permitted obvious criminals to walk away free or with lesser penalties, oftentimes due to technicalities.

Let me tell you what happened in this case in Texas. There were three charges. The suspect was found innocent of a sex-trafficking charge. But, he was found guilty of harboring a runaway minor and a sexual assault charge. He faces twenty years in jail. Will he serve it? Did the legal system work? Could it use reform? Why not take a look? What additional pain did it cause the teenage victim in court? Who knows?

Consider this: we need all the legal weapons we have to combat human trafficking. However, some present court procedures restrict their use. We should examine these restrictions and modify them. Sadly, people of all ages, all colors, all walks of life, single and married, are buying or renting the bodies of children, women, and men for coerced sex (rape) and forced labor (slavery).

Isn't it about time we come together to stop human trafficking? Here's what the average citizen can do against this seemingly unstoppable criminal activity:

1. Elect officials who will invest in strengthened law enforcement at local, state, federal, and international levels.
2. Arm law enforcement with superior legal weapons, tougher laws, and harsher courts.
3. Raise taxes as necessary to dismantle human trafficking across America and around the world.

We must end this evil business. Thousands of girls, boys, women, and men, too, will thank you.

SLAVERY IS HERE—DEEP IN THE HEART OF TEXAS

The US census of 1860 stated that black slaves were 30.2 percent of the population of Texas. I wonder what the percentage is today? Not only for black slaves but also for white slaves and sex slaves of many colors and ages, all trapped in the sordid business of human trafficking. At this moment, many Texans are trying to find out how prevalent modern slavery is in the Lone Star State.

Thanks to a $500,000 grant from the Criminal Justice Division of the governor's office in Austin, three groups of researchers have been working together since December 2014 to document the spread of slavery across the state. This two-year effort, known as the Texas Slavery Mapping Project, involves two departments of the University of Texas in Austin and Allies Against Slavery, an Austin nonprofit organization.

The university departments are the Institute on Domestic Violence & Sexual Assault (IDVSA), located in the School of Social Work, and the Bureau of Business Research (BBR), part of the IC2 Institute (Innovation, Creativity, and Capital Institute). The activities of the IC2 Institute include regional and global economic development among university, government, and private sectors.

The IDVSA focuses on interpersonal violence (i.e., human trafficking, sexual assault, stalking, domestic violence, and child abuse). The BBR analyzes and reports economic trends to help businesspeople and policymakers in their planning and decision-making. Allies Against Slavery seeks to disrupt human trafficking, including forced labor and coerced sex, in various Texas cities.

(Note: in 2013, data from Polaris, a nonprofit that operates the National Human Trafficking Hotline, showed that nearly one in eleven calls to the

hotline are from Texas—second only to California. Since this suggests that Texas is a target for traffickers, where's the bull's-eye? In Austin, Dallas-Fort Worth, El Paso, Houston, San Antonio? There may be several bull's-eyes scattered across this huge state.)

During the first year of the Texas Slavery Mapping Project, the three groups gathered data from district attorneys, local law enforcement, and state and national anti-trafficking organizations. They also created a catalog of services for trafficking victims, including legal advice, shelters, counseling, financial assistance, and job-skill development. The second year (2016) of the project is tracking slavery to several regions of the state, analyzing human and economic costs of slavery, and recommending legislation to combat it. (Earlier in this chapter, I mentioned California's Prop 35 and its stricter jail time. You might reread that information.)

Hopefully, new laws in Texas will be even tougher than California's. For example, depending on the age of a child rented or sold for sex, Texas might jail pimps and sex traffickers for a longer time than California does or might even consider capital punishment—just as that Utah lawmaker has proposed doing.

Stronger legal reform in the Lone Star State could send a message to pimps and human traffickers across America and around the world: **Don't mess with Texas; you're lucky if you *only* do time.**

CHAPTER 5

International Rape Culture

Countries that have been described as having "rape cultures" include Pakistan, India, the United States, the United Kingdom, Canada, Australia, and South Africa.
RAPE CULTURE, WIKIPEDIA

WHAT IS RAPE CULTURE?

IN 1963, BETTY FRIEDAN'S BEST-SELLING book, *The Feminine Mystique*, prepared the way for the second-wave feminist movement in America that viewed popular culture as sexist. The term *rape culture* was first coined in the 1970s by this movement that drew attention to domestic violence and marital rape, as well as the need for battered women's and rape crisis shelters. According to the *Encyclopedia of Rape* by Merril D. Smith, PhD, published 2004, the term rape culture characterized contemporary American culture. Amazon summarized this book on its website as follows:

"Rape has been perpetrated throughout history and worldwide, and today ours has been called a rape culture, because sexual violence, mainly against women and children, is prevalent and tolerated to some extent.

"The *Encyclopedia of Rape* offers 185 entries in an A-to-Z essay format covering the historical scope and magnitude of the issue in the United States and globally. Written by a host of scholars from diverse fields, it provides informed perspectives on the key dimensions of the topic, from concepts, social movements, offenders, high-profile cases, legislation, influential activists, landmark texts, and victimology to representations in literature and art."

For decades sociologists, psychologists, activists, feminists, writers, and others have tried to *define* rape culture by suggesting many of the following words: misogyny (hatred of women), sexual objectification, victim blaming, trivializing, normalizing, slut-shaming, legal apathy, media perpetuation, sexist jokes, mainstream acceptance, et al.

Perhaps we are trying too hard. Why not a simplified definition, such as the one summarized above by Amazon? For ease of reading, I'll repeat it here in Bold Face type:

Rape has been perpetrated throughout history and worldwide, and today ours has been called a rape culture, because sexual violence, mainly against women and children, is prevalent and tolerated to some extent.

The preceding chapter (Chapter 4) discussed violence against women in film, on TV and in rap lyrics. You might want to reread it. In addition to this information, studies from the United Nations and the US National Crime Victimization Survey (NCVS, 2009–2013) have already told us about rape culture—approximately 80 percent of rapes are committed by someone *known* to the victim, 47 percent of rapists are *friends* or *acquaintances*, and 5 percent of rapists are *relatives*. Eighteen percent of rapes are by *strangers,* according to the US Department of Justice.

Let's review this finding:

80 percent of rapes are by someone known to the victim.
47 percent of rapes are by a friend or acquaintance.
5 percent of rapes are by relatives.
18 percent of rapes are by strangers.

Would you have believed that 80 percent of the rapes in America are by someone known to the victims? Aren't strangers responsible for most rapes? No. While rape by strangers dominates the headlines, rape by all kinds of "friends" is seldom known or reported by media. These males—who can't keep their pants zipped up—are violating females they know. In addition to physically and psychologically harming someone they know, these males put themselves in jeopardy.

Should they rape someone under the age of sixteen, they might spend years in jail. After they are released, they might have to register as sex offenders forever, wherever they live. This kind of information might be sought on an employment application or on a college or university application for admission. Who would hire them? Who would permit them on campus? What kind of life would they have left? They could forfeit their future for a few moments of sexual aggression and ejaculatory relief.

Types of Rape

In the introduction of this book, I suggested that slavery began when battlefield winners stopped killing losers and decided to enslave them for unpaid work (slavery) and coerced sex (rape). Rape was common in the ancient world. Now, as then, some men rape avidly. In war or peace, some men rape to feel powerful whether they are warlords, soldiers, slave owners, pimps, gang members, acquaintances, dates, friends, classmates, or relatives.

Conquering armies—Greek, Roman, others—engaged in war rape. Once they took a town by force, they killed or enslaved defeated men and raped women and youths. Warlords raped and encouraged their warriors to rape, as the men anticipated a sexual reward for winning an easy victory or hard-fought battle. Some military commanders throughout history permitted soldiers to rape with impunity in order to terrorize and demoralize a defeated foe. (Other leaders, such as Napoleon Bonaparte, despised rape and ordered that anyone guilty of rape be shot.)

Some slave owners in the American South raped black slaves because they could, despite bitter protests from white wives who felt betrayed and humiliated in front of family, friends, and neighbors. But wives had very little to say, since they were considered the property of husbands, similar to slaves. The South and North were, as now, patriarchal societies in early America; today our male-dominated society also extends from the east coast to the west coast.

Gang members hunt in packs (like hyenas) to assure safety and strength in numbers while seeking vulnerable prey to rape. Some husbands rape when drunk, on drugs, when feeling powerless at work, or when unemployed. Friends, cousins, and classmates rape after they convince girls they are trusted males, when they are not. From time immemorial, men have raped to subjugate and ejaculate, to sate their id and negate their superego—the conscience of the self.

Here are several categories from a *Wikipedia* entry (with forty-two sources) titled Types of Rape: *date* rape, which could involve drugs; *gang* rape, involving two or more predators; *spousal* rape, due to several reasons; rape of *children* by a person of authority or family member; *statutory* rape, when the victim is below a certain age; *prison* rape, affecting up to 12 percent of inmates in US prisons; *revenge* rape, specific to certain cultures; *war* rape, mentioned above; *corrective* rape, a form of hate crime against LGBT individuals; *custodial* rape by a person of authority in a public or private facility. As stated earlier, rape by a *stranger* accounts for approximately 18 percent of sexual assaults, according to the US Department of Justice.

Rapes Recently Reported in the News

Ten ISIS Members Gang-Rape Nine-Year-Old Yazidi Girl. In April 2015, ten members of ISIS took turns gang-raping a nine-year-old Yazidi girl, captured as a sex slave. She was traumatized, became pregnant. It was an act of modern war rape against a non-Muslim by formerly futureless males, now ISIS killers and rapists. ISIS uses these methods to terrorize a defeated foe and teach systematic brutality to its members. Many females have been beaten, raped repeatedly, and forced to convert to Islam.

Boko Haram Members Rape Hundreds of Female Captives in Nigeria. In May 2015, reports revealed that hundreds of girls and women enslaved by Boko Haram have been subjected to war rape intended to humiliate, intimidate, and impregnate. Boko Haram and ISIS have used sexual violence to spread terror among many groups that do not embrace their ideology. UNICEF (the United Nations's children's fund) has reported that Boko Haram has displaced 800,000 children due to violence.

Teenage Sex Slave Is Raped 43,200 Times in Four Years. In November 2015, CNN reported on yet another human-trafficking victim: snared at age twelve, saved at age sixteen. Four years of hell: 30 johns a day (how many married?), 7 days a week, 1,460 days of sex slavery, 35,040 hours of degradation, 43,200 rapes. She could have been someone you know; she could have been your sister; she could have been you.

Rape Kits and Rape Exams

You know the drill: "She said; he said." Decades ago, "he said" usually won in court, thanks to male cops, male judges, and male attack-dog lawyers whose main interest was to rape the victim again, verbally this time. How many girls were damaged psychologically in court after they had been violated physically? How many parents felt guilty because they had failed to protect their daughters? How many rapists should have gone to jail? We will never know.

But we do know this: According to the US Justice Department in 2014, there were 400,000 untested rape kits gathering dust for years in police department evidence-storage facilities from Portland, Maine, to Portland, Oregon; from Minneapolis to Miami; from San Diego to San Antonio; from Detroit to Denver. The list goes on and on. Unanalyzed. Ignored. A mere 400,000 examples of females being slighted as second-class citizens by the law's officials. Does this inaction confirm rape culture?

Enter the Joyful Heart Foundation (JHF) and its persistent effort to identify the number of untested rape kits across the United States. On May 19, 2015, JHF provided new data on rape-kit backlogs in five US cities: Charlotte, NC, 1,019 kits; Jacksonville, FL, 1,943 kits; Kansas City, MO, 1,324 kits; Portland, OR, 1,931 kits; and San Diego, CA, 2,873 kits.

This data is part of the Accountability Project, JHF's ENDTHEBACKLOG program to uncover the extent of the rape-kit backlog in cities across America. In pro bono partnership with two law firms—Goodwin Procter LLP and Weil, Gotshal & Manges LLP—the initiative uses public records requests to determine the number of untested kits at police departments around the country. Since few states and no federal agencies require law enforcement to track or count untested rape kits in storage, the Accountability Project seeks to bring more transparency and responsibility to rape-kit testing practices nationwide.

"Testing rape kits sends a fundamental and critical message to victims of sexual violence," said Maile M. Zambuto, Joyful Heart's Chief Executive Officer. "You matter. What happened to you matters."

Here is information about rape kits provided by RAINN (Rape, Abuse & Incest National Network), one of America's largest anti-sexual-assault organizations.

A rape kit may also be referred to as:

- sexual assault evidence collection kit
- sexual assault forensic evidence (SAFE) kit
- sexual offense evidence collection (SOEC) kit
- physical evidence recovery kit (PERK)

Following sexual assault, a victim has the opportunity of going to a hospital to have a forensic examination by a trained professional. This person might be a sexual assault nurse examiner (SANE) or forensic examiner who has received specialized training. The rape kit offers an orderly way of collecting DNA that may have been left by the suspect. Although the contents of the rape kit may vary by state or jurisdiction, it usually includes instructions, bags and sheets for evidence collection, swabs, comb, envelopes, blood collection devices, and documentation forms.

Let's review and restate the value of the rape kit: **The rape kit offers an orderly way of collecting DNA that may have been left by the suspect.**

An examination discovers the predator's DNA, protects it, and stores it in the rape kit. When the DNA is analyzed and the FBI's Combined

Index System, or CODIS, is searched, suspects can be caught and jailed. Here are examples of the system working:

In 2009, Detroit officials unearthed more than 11,000 untested rape kits, some over twenty years old. An analysis of the first 1,600 kits pinpointed 455 suspects in 23 states with 87 connected to multiple assaults.

In Cuyahoga County, Ohio (which includes Cleveland), a cache of about 4,000 rape kits, accumulating since the early 1990s, was forwarded to the state lab for testing. Bingo: 173 suspects have been indicted, with 38 accused of multiple rapes.

But don't rejoice too soon.

In 2012 in New York City, a rapist, whose DNA connected him with three brutal sex attacks, was freed on a technicality. Due to a rape-kit backlog, the police filed charges *one day* after the statute of limitations had expired. The rapist taunted the police. His lawyer declined comment. People might wonder—if the lawyer has a daughter and she is raped by a similar serial rapist freed on a technicality—what would he say to her?

"Get over it?"

THREE WAYS YOU CAN CHANGE RAPE CULTURE IN AMERICA

ONE: HELP DISCOVER UNTESTED RAPE KITS

The discovery of 400,000 untested rape kits verifies the existence of rape culture (some kits have been sitting somewhere out of sight and out of mind for twenty years or more!). The 400,000 rape kits outnumber the US Census Bureau's 2015 estimate of population for New Orleans, or Cleveland, or Tulsa. Finding these kits is just a start. More will be found; more rapists hunted down. Here's how you can help.

Bring Justice to Victims in Your Community. Thanks to the Joyful Heart Foundation (JHF) and others, the rape kit backlog is being reduced nationwide. Kits analyzed; rapists jailed. Children, women, and men saved from future rape. The process of discovering rapists will continue for years. You can help ENDTHEBACKLOG of rape kits in your community; please contact *joyfulheartfoundation.org*. Help each other.

TWO: STOP RAPISTS FROM BEING FREED ON TECHNICALITIES
When DNA verifies rape suspects, they should be jailed and not freed due to a technicality, such as the expiration of a statute of limitations. Never again.

End Statutes of Limitations for Rape. Although twenty-seven states, as of August 31, 2013, have some form of DNA exception that extends the time limit for prosecuting a rape, that's not good enough. The entire statute of limitations should be repealed. On June 2, 2015, Mona Manglona, writing for the *Digital Voice,* a publication of Philadelphia University's Law and Society Program, posted this point of view: "Murder does not have a statute of limitations, why should rape, a heinous act that ruins the life of a person have a deadline? Sex crimes should not have a statute of limitations, because there is no statute of limitations to a victim's suffering. Rape is an unjustifiable crime that should not come with an expiration date, thus the statute of limitations on sex crimes should be eliminated in all 50 states."

Be Proactive. If a statute of limitations (SOL) on rape exists in your state, urge that it be repealed. Contact every legislator, including the governor. Tell them about the Joyful Heart Foundation. Involve your daily and weekly newspaper, also, TV and radio. Show officials and members of the press how they can help put rapists in jail.

If some legislators and governors refuse to repeal the SOL, make sure they are identified with supporting the rapists—pimps, johns, human traffickers, others. Their unwillingness to act encourages rape of children; elect people who will save children and women from rape—not those who stand by and do nothing.

THREE: SUPPORT THOSE TRYING TO CHANGE A MALE MIND-SET
Too many men remain silent when they hear rape jokes. Some are afraid to intervene when they see a rape about to happen. Inaction helps rape culture spread. Fortunately, there are organizations that teach boys and men how to end sexual assault and violence against women.

Male Mentors Reverse Male Mind-Set. Here are three organizations that are working to change the male mind-set of seeing females as only sex objects and rape targets. You may know of some of these groups; work with them.

1. A Call to Men: This organization was created out of a battered women's movement in 2002. The founders—Tony Porter and Ted Bunch—believe that preventing domestic and sexual violence is primarily the responsibility of men; men should stand up and speak out against all forms of violence and discrimination against women and girls.

Over the past ten years, A Call to Men has helped more than 100,000 people, including more than 30,000 men and boys, understand how healthy and honorable manhood can prevent domestic and sexual violence. The organization's training teams have worked with hundreds of sports organizations, high schools, and colleges throughout the country. These colleges include Harvard, Columbia, Morehouse, Berkeley, and the military academies of West Point and Annapolis.

A Call to Men has trained men and women from over 3,000 organizations in America, including hundreds of national, state, local, and community-based groups. Gloria Steinem made the following observation about A Call to Men: "There is no doubt that these men and this organization are a key component in engaging men's participation and responsibility to ending violence against women."

2. Men Stopping Violence: For more than thirty years, this group has persisted in working to create an environment of safety and justice for women and children. The late Kathleen Carlin, executive director of the Cobb County, Georgia, YMCA Women's Resource Center, hired two Atlanta therapists in 1981 to get batterers of women to open up and talk on tape about the ways they viewed and treated women.

The therapists—Dick Bathrick, MA, and Gus Kaufman Jr., PhD—and Ms. Carlin learned that men were more likely to change when they were continually reminded of the impact of their actions on women in their lives. Within a year, they realized it was time to form an organization whose mission engaged men in ending violence against women.

In 1982, Men Stopping Violence (MSV) was incorporated as a non-profit with Congressman John Lewis as its first president. By 1994, Kathleen, Gus, and Dick had become convinced that social change was the key to preventing violence against women. That year MSV received an award from the Centers for Disease Control and Prevention (CDC) to conduct research into effective community interaction to end battering. Today, MSV's mission of building safe communities for women and girls is made possible with hundreds of hours of volunteer time and financial donations from corporations, foundations, supporters, and friends.

3. Men Can Stop Rape: Founded in 1997, this organization has a mission not only to mobilize men to use their strength for creating cultures free of violence, but also to stop violence before it happens. This approach is grounded in CDC's four-level social-ecological model, which addresses many factors likely to reduce violence over time. (To learn more about this model, see CDC's Principles of Prevention online.)

Men Can Stop Rape has reached more than two million young people and professionals with its award-winning youth program known as the MOST (Men Of Strength) Club. MOST reaches young people ages eleven to eighteen and teaches healthy dating-relationship skills. Now in its eleventh year, MOST's middle and high school curriculum is taught in over one hundred schools in the District of Columbia, New York City, and the states of California, Florida, Kansas, Maryland, Missouri, North Carolina, Ohio, and South Carolina. The MOST Club has eight chapters on college campuses in Washington DC, Florida, Hawaii, New York, and North Carolina.

Men Can Stop Rape has joined with the *NO MORE project to increase awareness of domestic violence and sexual assault in communities across America. To get involved, contact MenCanStopRape.org or nomore.org.

(These "thumbnail" profiles are based on postings from the websites of the organizations. The organizations mentioned are representative of numerous fine groups dedicated to the elimination of profit-driven human trafficking and all types of rape.)

---

* NO MORE is a unifying symbol and campaign, launched in March 2013, to raise public awareness and engage people in ending domestic violence and sexual assault. Join this public/private partnership with the US Department of Justice and thousands of citizens. To learn more, visit nomore.org.

CONCLUSION

Right Makes Might

THE FBI; LOCAL, STATE, REGIONAL, and global law enforcement; our courts; and some of our state legislatures are leading the fight to end human trafficking. Thousands of children, women, and men, once caught in the international sex trade, are now free. Pimps and human traffickers are spending more time in jail than they ever imagined. So are johns. But, there is a lot more to do. The business of sex slavery is not easily overcome. Average citizens can help by electing officials at all levels of government who seek to defeat human trafficking, the world's third largest criminal activity.

Meanwhile, numerous groups are attempting to change America's rape culture by reversing a male mind-set toward girls and women. Reeducation is helping this effort. Many Americans have declared NO MORE. You can, too. This chapter has given you three ways to participate. Please choose one. Thank you.

EPILOGUE

Human Trafficking aka Slavery, Rape, Greed

IN A SENSE, WE ARE back where we began our journey of discovery. Not much has changed in 7,000 years in terms of human behavior. That's disheartening as well as unacceptable. But, we can turn disillusionment into action. Citizens and cops in California did with Prop 35. FBI and police officers across our country did in arresting pimps and freeing children. The US Department of Justice did with unearthing 400,000 untested rape kits and the Joyful Heart Foundation gladly accepted the chance to identify those rape kits across our country. There is much to be done and many are eager to help.

In America and around the world many groups are trying to end slavery and rape. Sometimes these good people may seem to be shoveling sand against an endless tide of inhumanity. Yet they persist in doing difficult, honorable work day after day.

May they continue; may they succeed; and may God bless them, every one.

SELECTED BIBLIOGRAPHY

Human Trafficking: From 5000 BC to the 21st Century

Barber, James. *Eyewitness Books: Presidents.* New York: Dorling Kindersley, 2000.

Benson, Kathleen, and James Haskins. *Africa: A Look Back.* Tarrytown, NY: Marshall Cavendish Benchmark, 2007.

Blauer, Ettagale, and Jason Laure. *Enchantment of the World: Mozambique.* Chicago: Children's Press, 1995.

Boorstin, Daniel J. *The Discoverers.* New York: Random House, 1983.

Brownmiller, Susan. *Against Our Will: Men, Women, and Rape.* New York: Simon & Schuster, 1975.

Carter, Jimmy. *A Call to Action: Women, Religion, Violence, and Power.* New York: Simon & Schuster, 2014.

Corrick, James A. *World History Series: The Early Middle Ages.* San Diego: Lucent Books, 1995.

Cullen-DuPont, Kathryn. *Human Trafficking.* New York: Facts on File, An imprint of Infobase Publishing, 2009.

Curtin, Philip, Steven Feierman, Leonard Thompson, and Jan Vansina. *African History: From Earliest Times to Independence.* 2nd ed. London: Longman Group Limited, 1995.

Dewey, Susan, and Patty Kelly, eds. *Policy Pleasure*. New York: New York University Press, 2011.

Ellis, Joseph J. *Founding Brothers*. New York: Alfred A. Knopf, 2001.

Garlan, Yvon. *Slavery in Ancient Greece*. Ithaca, NY: Cornell University Press, 1988.

Glancy, Jennifer A. *Slavery in Early Christianity*. Oxford: Oxford University Press, 2002.

Hopkins, Keith. *Conquerors and Slaves*. Sociological Studies in Roman History, vol. 1. Cambridge: Cambridge University Press, 1978.

Hornblower, Simon, and Antony Spawforth, eds. *The Oxford Companion to Classical Civilizations*. Oxford: Oxford University Press, 1998.

Laure, Jason. *Enchantment of the World: Angola*. Chicago: Children's Press, 1990.

Lovejoy, Paul E. *Transformations in Slavery*. Cambridge: Cambridge University Press, 1983.

Manning, Patrick. *Slavery and African Life*. Cambridge: Cambridge University Press, 1990.

———. *The African Diaspora*. New York: Columbia University Press, 2009.

McKissack, Patricia C., and Frederick L. McKissack. *Rebels against Slavery*. New York: Scholastic Press, 1996.

Meltzer, Milton. *All Times, All Peoples: A World History of Slavery*. New York: Harper and Row, 1980.

———. *Slavery: A World History*. New York: Da Capo Press, 1993.

Milton, Giles. *White Gold*. New York: Farrar, Straus and Giroux, 2004.

Morris, Richard B. *Founding Fathers*. New York: HarperCollins, 1976.

O'Neill, Amanda. *Ancient Times: A Journey from the Dawn of History to the Glory of Rome*. New York: Crescent Books, 1992.

Rothman, Adam. *Slave Country*. Cambridge, MA: Harvard University Press, 2007.

Sage, Jesse, and Liora Kasten, eds. *Enslaved: True Stories of Modern Day Slavery*. With a foreword by Gloria Steinem. New York: Palgrave Macmillan, 2006.

Segal, Ronald. *Islam's Black Slaves*. New York: Farrar, Straus and Giroux, 2001.

Shelley, Louise. *Human Trafficking, A Global Perspective*. New York: Cambridge University Press, 2010.

Stearman, Kaye. *Slavery Today*. Austin, TX: Raintree Steck-Vaughn Publishers, 2000.

Stearns, Peter N., gen. ed. *The Encyclopedia of World History*. Boston: Houghton Mifflin Company, 2001.

Thomas, Hugh. *The Slave Trade*. New York: Simon & Schuster, 1997.

Urbainczyk, Theresa. *Slave Revolts in Antiquity*. Berkeley, CA: University of California Press, 2008.

Watkins, Richard. *Slavery Bondage throughout History*. Boston: Houghton Mifflin Company, 2001.

Wiedeman, Thomas. *Greek and Roman Slavery*. Baltimore: The Johns Hopkins University Press, 1981.

Wright, John. *The Trans-Saharan Slave Trade*. Abingdon, UK: Routledge, 2007.

Acknowledgements

Thanks to Heather and Jeff for their insightful observations and suggestions. As a result, may more children, women and men be saved today from slavery and rape; may more pimps and sex traffickers be jailed in America and around the world. Someday, may human trafficking be ended, forever.

About the Author

AFTER FORTY-PLUS YEARS WORKING IN journalism, advertising, and publishing, K. G. Richardson decided to put this professional experience toward a truly good cause.

An interest in the historical and sociological causes of slavery, rape, and greed turned into a passion to know and understand the causes of human trafficking today—and a desire to inform and educate others on how they can use their own lives to put an end to this evil and all too prevalent practice.

Made in the USA
Las Vegas, NV
22 October 2024

10276611R00069